D1093980

THE INSPIRATION OF SCRIPTURE

The Inspiration of Scripture

by
Dewey M. Beegle

THE WESTMINSTER PRESS
Philadelphia

LIBRARY OF CONGRESS CATALOG CARD NO. 63-7342

PUBLISHED BY THE WESTMINSTER PRESS®
PHILADELPHIA 7, PENNSYLVANIA

PRINTED IN THE UNITED STATES OF AMERICA

To my wife

MARION

without whose love and encouragement
this book would not have been written

Contents

Preface

There are few areas of Christian life and thought that do not lead back eventually to the issue of the inspiration of Scripture. Sooner or later, therefore, every generation of Christians is confronted with the necessity of determining what it believes with respect to this doctrine and to the related issues of revelation and authority. Today, ministers and inquiring laymen of conservative, evangelical Protestantism are especially cognizant of this confrontation. It is generally acknowledged that the findings and convictions of the past, valid as they may have been, cannot be the answer for this generation unless they can withstand reexamination in the light of new information gained during the last forty years or so. The purpose of this book is to make such a reexamination.

All the relevant data possible, both Biblical and non-Biblical, will be reckoned with, in order to ascertain the truth of the matter concerning the inspiration of Scripture. The author has tried to write simply and to deal with issues that are foremost in the thinking of ministers and alert laymen. Accordingly, theological and philosophical implications are considered in conjunction with the attempt to discuss the extent, types, and results of inspiration. Notwithstanding the desire to eliminate as much technical data as possible, a few of the key issues involve some very complex material. There is no easy path to truth, and apparently the problem of inspiration is no exception.

The footnotes, consisting largely of references to sources cited or quoted in the text, have been grouped together, according to chapters, at the end of the book. Furthermore, a bibliography of books and articles consulted has been included along with the Scriptural and general indexes.

The writer wishes to express his gratitude to Edwin H. Rian, Ralph W. Key, and Robert A. Traina, colleagues at The Biblical Seminary, for checking the manuscript at its various stages and for offering constructive criticisms. Thanks are also due the following for reading and commenting on some or all of the various manuscript revisions: Robert G. Bratcher, F. F. Bruce, Jacob Enz, Charles Farah, John Graybill, J. Harold Greenlee, Paul Hopkins, Walden Howard, Paul K. Jewett, J. Laurence Kulp, Herbert Livingston, Charles Pfeiffer, Bernard L. Ramm, Claude Thompson, and George A. Turner. In the last analysis, however, the writer must assume responsibility for the ideas incorporated.

Special expressions of appreciation are due Mrs. Astrid Ohanian and Mrs. Naomi Hansen for their assistance in typing the various revisions.

D. M. B.

New York City

1: *The Problem of Method*

When Christians claim that the Bible is inspired they generally mean at least two things: (1) explicitly, the canonical writings are the result of God's making himself known "in many and various ways," and (2) implicitly, without God's initiative and activity the collection of books that we call Scripture would never have come into existence. Tradition has expressed these convictions in the statement, "The Bible is God's Word."

However, history has shown that Christians can agree on this generalization and yet have quite divergent interpretations as to what it means when translated into specific details. Clearly, then, our first problem is to determine the most accurate means for ascertaining the truest interpretation of the data relevant to the doctrine of inspiration. Without question the most crucial factor is that of method.

Deduction and Induction

The human mind is capable of two basic processes of reasoning. One of these is the *deductive* method. It starts with an assumption or generalization from which are deduced details or particulars. The other approach is the *inductive* method. It begins with facts or details from which a generalization or principle is formulated.

The two methods of reasoning are well illustrated by archaeology. In excavating an ancient mound (*tell*) with its many layers of superimposed cities, the primary task is to dig down through these various strata, labeling all the objects according to the stratum in which they were discovered. When these facts are correlated the archaeologist observes that the pottery, for example, of a certain stratum has form and features about it that distinguish it from the pottery of other strata. In other words, each stratum tends to have its own type or class of pottery. This process of observation and inductive reasoning from facts to generalization is called "stratigraphy."

On the other hand, when the archaeologist comes across the same type of pottery while excavating another mound he makes the deduction that the stratum in which the pottery was found dates from the same general period as the similar stratum in the first mound. This deductive reasoning from the generalization of pottery form to certain facts about the pottery is called "typology."

The accurate archaeological results of the last four decades have resulted from careful application of both of these methods of reasoning, and it has become increasingly apparent that adequate solutions to any other complex problems necessitate both induction and deduction. If handled properly, therefore, the two methods are complementary: a valid deduction should result in details that accord with the observable facts, and correct observation and relating of details should lead to a sound generalization.

Although granting the propriety and necessity of both kinds of reasoning, this does not mean that one is free to begin resolving the problem with whichever method happens to strike one's fancy at the moment. Sound results are obtained when induction precedes deduction. The history of archaeological activity makes this quite evident. Early attempts at interpreting the data often led to conflicting conclusions because the assumptions of certain archaeologists either distorted their observation of the facts or made it impossible for them to detect some of the pertinent details. Order came out of chaos when priority was given to inductive reasoning, and the same can be said for all other realms of science.

In the early stages of the struggle between science and Christianity, the church in general shied away from the inductive method on the grounds that it was not applicable to the realm of Scripture and theology. In the twentieth century, however, the church has become increasingly aware of the fact that God is the author of all truth and, accordingly, that the priority of induction is equally valid in the study of Scripture.

The Priority of Faith

At this juncture a clarification is in order. By induction we do ***not*** mean an investigation of Scripture to determine whether or not we will believe its message. Some have found Christ in this way, but for the vast majority of Christians the act of faith preceded any systematic attempts to determine the validity and meaning of Scripture. In this study, therefore, the expression " priority of induction " means that induction is the first method of reasoning to be employed in the interpretation of the Bible. This definition implies the prior act of faith and commitment to God and his revelation. The author frankly acknowledges his genuine belief in the inspiration and authority of Scripture, and he assumes that his readers share this conviction. Aside from the ultimate authority of the triune God, Scripture is our highest authority and to it we must defer in our search for God's revelation and will for us. By the inductive method, then, we mean a reverent approach to Scripture that resolves at all costs to let God's Word speak for itself.

Application of Method

Few Christian leaders dissent from this basic principle of interpretation. In fact, most interpreters of Scripture claim to be inductive in their method of study. Notwithstanding this unanimity on method the results are often widely divergent. Evidently the basic problem lies more in the area of application of method. Theoretical assent to the priority of inductive reasoning is no assurance of its actualization in practice. Accordingly, any study on the doctrine of inspiration that expects to approximate the truth of the matter must be characterized by two features: accurate observation of the data and specific consideration of all the data.

It is recognized that the Biblical writers did not set forth their view of inspiration with the detail and completeness of systematic theologians, but insofar as they expressed themselves in this regard their statements are primary data for consideration. Every claim they make for their inspiration is a relevant fact and so is every statement concerning the topic of inspiration.

On the other hand, any attempt to let Scripture speak for itself necessarily involves more than the teaching or doctrinal statements of the Biblical writers. One must also reckon with the facts (sometimes referred to as "phenomena") of the Biblical record. Included in this category are such considerations as the correlation of historical details noted in Scripture with the non-Biblical data, and also the manner in which the New Testament writers quoted and referred to the Old Testament. A truly Biblical formulation of inspiration must give equal weight to the teaching and to the facts of Scripture.

General Views of Inspiration

Failure to deal with the whole body of Biblical data has resulted in some general, but more or less one-sided, definitions of inspiration. One extreme example is the view that characterizes inspiration as *intuition* — an inspired person is the religious genius who has a talent for spiritual insight. Thus the Biblical writers were merely gifted men who were distinguished from their contemporaries only by their keener natural insight into truth.

This definition may account for Luke's claim with respect to his historical investigations, but it discounts completely the claims of Moses and the prophets. True inductive reasoning must also account for the conviction of Jeremiah, for example, that "the word of the LORD" became for him "a reproach and derision all day long" (ch. 20:8). When he resolved not to speak again the name of the LORD there arose within him "a burning fire," as it were, which made it impossible for him to be silent any longer. This kind of inspiration was far more than heightened natural insight. The God of Israel was at work here.

Another general view defines inspiration as *illumination* — the person who has a deep experience with God is inspired. On this theory the Spirit of God is active in the Biblical writer, but it is essentially an intensification of that illumination which is common to all followers of God. A number of passages in Scripture can be explained by this view, but it too is an oversimplification that cannot account adequately for the very personal, dynamic experiences of Isaiah and Jeremiah, for example.

An opposite extreme from the intuition view defines inspiration in terms of *dictation* — the inspired person is one to whom the Holy Spirit dictates the precise words of God's message. This mechanical concept of inspiration was held by a few of the ancients, both Jews and Christians. Some formulations of inspiration made since the Reformation have been criticized by others as teaching the dictation view, but in each instance the author (or his disciples) has denied the charge. Perhaps the clearest evidence in support of this view is found in Ex. 31:18; the two tables of testimony were written "with the finger of God." This anthropomorphism, regardless of how one interprets it, implies that God communicated the precise words directly. But to conceive of this rare event as God's usual method of revelation is an unwarranted assumption. An inductive approach to the Biblical data indicates clearly that as a general rule God's servants were alert and in control of all their faculties during the process of communication.

A fourth general definition is the so-called *dynamic* view of inspiration — the inspired person has the extraordinary help of the Holy Spirit without violating his individuality and personality. The mass of Christians have held to this view because it accounts for the greater part of the Biblical data; but even so, it is not the complete answer to the problem of inspiration.

The Biblical teaching and data relevant to the issue of inspiration are so complex and many-faceted that it is virtually impossible to formulate the doctrine of inspiration in any concise, general statement. In this study, therefore, the various aspects of the problem will be treated topically, after which an attempt will be made to formulate a view consistent with the greatest amount of the relevant data.

2: *Inspiration and the Autographs*

For more than a century now the autographs, the original text of the various Biblical books, have figured prominently in any major discussion of the doctrine of inspiration. It is imperative, therefore, that we learn what Scripture itself has to say on this important issue.

The Autograph of Jeremiah

The most detailed account of the origin of a Biblical book is found in Jer. 36:1-32. In the fourth year of Jehoiakim (605 B.C.) the LORD told Jeremiah, "Take a scroll and write on it all the words that I have spoken to you against Israel and Judah and all the nations from the day I spoke to you, from the days of Josiah until today" (v. 2). Jeremiah called his scribe, or secretary (known technically as an "amanuensis"), Baruch, who "wrote upon a scroll at the dictation of Jeremiah all the words of the LORD which he had spoken to him" (v. 4).

Inasmuch as Jeremiah had been debarred from going to the Temple, he ordered Baruch to read the scroll to the people on some fast day. This Baruch did (v. 10); whereupon a certain Micaiah, one of the officials, hearing the startling words of Jeremiah, reported what he heard to the princes who were sitting in the king's house. They sent for Baruch and had him read the scroll to them (vs. 14-15). In fear they reported to the king, who in turn asked to have the scroll read to him. Since it was winter, he happened to be warming himself before the fire in the brazier. Then "as Jehudi read three or four columns, the king would cut them off with a penknife and throw them into the fire in the brazier, until the entire scroll was consumed in the fire that was in the brazier" (v. 23).

The scroll must have been much shorter than our present text, because it was read three times, with intervals, apparently all on the same day. At any rate, after Jeremiah learned of the burning of the scroll, the LORD told him, "Take another scroll and write on it all the former words that were in the first scroll" (v. 28). Then "Jeremiah took another scroll and gave it to Baruch the scribe, . . . who wrote on it at the dictation of Jeremiah all the words of the scroll which Jehoiakim king of Judah had burned in the fire; and many similar words were added to them" (v. 32).

Some of the additional words were the oracle (included in our present book at ch. 36:29-31) against King Jehoiakim for his shameless deed in burning the first scroll. However, the text says "many similar words were added," so the second scroll (written in 604) was quite a bit longer than the first. On the other hand, this second scroll was much shorter than our present book of Jeremiah, for it did not contain the material dating from 604 to the fall of Jerusalem, 587/6 B.C.; nor did it have the section, chs. 43:8 to 44:30, which reports Jeremiah's activities in Egypt sometime after 586 B.C. When the latter unit was added, the preface of Jeremiah (ch. 1:1-3) was not brought up to date because it only purports to give the "words of Jeremiah . . . until the captivity of Jerusalem."

The differences between the text of Jeremiah in the Hebrew (known as the Masoretic text, or MT) and in the Greek translation of the Hebrew known as the Septuagint (meaning "seventy," and commonly designated LXX) indicate clearly that the book is a collection of materials, some of which circulated as separate units before being incorporated into the collection. An excellent example is the unit composed of chs. 46 to 51, a book of oracles against the nations, which appears in the Septuagint after ch. 25:13a. In this process of an enlarging prophetic collection or anthology, what is the autograph? Inasmuch as the Hebrew text of Jeremiah available in Jesus' day was essentially the same in extent as our present Hebrew copies, it would seem advisable to define the autograph as the original scroll that corresponded in *extent* to the traditional, canonical compilation. To do otherwise would necessitate deleting portions of the text as having no rightful place in the book, but from our vantage point it would be impossible to determine precisely what to omit.

If the average Christian today were asked to define an autograph, the most likely answer would be, "The book that came from the hand of the author." This definition springs from an assumption that the original text of each Biblical book was written at a certain time by the author. While this may have been true in some cases, it is not even the general rule in the New Testament. Aside from Paul's closing greeting and signature, most (if not all) of his letters were given by dictation (II Thess. 3:17; Gal. 6:11). Strictly speaking, then, the original letters of Paul involved the activity of various scribes. Here, as in the case of Jeremiah, the question is whether scribes, as well as authors, were preserved from error. It may have been so, but there is no evidence for it.

Scriptural Claims About the Autographs

In addition to the data of Scripture concerning the origin of Biblical books it is also necessary to ascertain if there are any specific claims or clear implications by Jesus and the New Testament writers concerning the autographs.

An excellent starting point for this inductive study is the classic statement on inspiration found in II Tim. 3:16-17. The passage begins, "All Scripture *theopneustos*." The Greek word transliterated *theopneustos* occurs nowhere else in the New Testament and only a few times in the Greek literature extant. The King James Version translates, "All Scripture is given by inspiration of God," and the Revised Standard Version reads similarly, "All scripture is inspired by God." The American Standard Version of 1901 has, "Every scripture inspired of God is . . . ," while the New English Bible translates, "Every inspired scripture has . . . ." Thus the major translations into English interpret *theopneustos* to mean "given by inspiration of God," or "inspired [by God]." The term has also been interpreted to mean "God-breathed."[1]

The word "scripture" (Greek, "*graphē*") seems to refer back to the previous sentence in vs. 14-15: "But as for you, continue in what you have learned and have firmly believed, knowing from whom you learned it and how from childhood you have been acquainted with the sacred writings which are able to instruct you for salvation through faith in Christ Jesus." Scripture, however, does more than prepare for salvation. It completes the man of God by teaching, reproof, correction, and training in righteousness. Therefore, the "sacred writings" which instructed Timothy in the past will continue to guide him as he matures in his Christian experience. It would appear, then, that for Paul the "scripture" and the "sacred writings" meant the extant Old Testament manuscripts.

The Greek text of vs. 16-17 is verbless, but since English idiom demands a verb all the translations into English supply "is" or "has." The clear implication of Paul's claim is that *theopneustos* is a permanent attribute of Scripture. The extant manuscripts were considered the same as the original writings because they were inspired by God and capable of accomplishing the purpose for which they were given. In all likelihood Paul never thought in terms of the technical distinction between the autographs and copies of Scripture. More important, however, is the fact that he never makes any claims nor proposes any definitions that would set the original writings apart as a special group to be clearly distinguished from copies of Scripture.

Another key passage on the doctrine of inspiration is the statement of Jesus as found in John 10:34-36: "Is it not written in your law, 'I said, you are gods'? If he called them gods to whom the word of God came (and scripture cannot be broken), do you say of him whom the Father consecrated and sent into the world, 'You are blaspheming,' because I said, 'I am the Son of God'?" Here Jesus is refuting his Jewish adversaries and so he refers to their copies of the Old Testament as "your law." By quoting from their manuscripts of Ps. 82:6, Jesus is establishing a common ground for discussion.

The question as to what Jesus meant by "broken" will be considered in another context. The important question here is to ascertain which "scripture" Jesus had in mind as having this characteristic. Did he mean "the word of God" which came to the gods (apparently a reference to the judges of Israel), or did he have in mind the Old Testament writings common to himself and his Jewish adversaries? The message or instructions that the judges received from God would constitute at best only a small portion of the Old Testament. What Jesus is stressing in this context is that the statement as written in Ps. 82:6 of the extant scrolls is authoritative. After all, his whole argument rests on this verse. The reason this verse is authoritative is that the entire context, the Old Testament Scriptures, can withstand any test. The Greek text of Jesus' qualification reads literally, "And the writing is not able to be broken." It does not say, "And the writing could not be broken." Therefore the text and the context seem to inform us that Jesus was arguing for the authority of the Old Testament writings common to himself and his adversaries. It is implied, of course, that Jesus thought as highly of the autographs, but this is not his explicit concern in this passage.

Peter, in his second letter, disputes the idea that Jesus was a "cleverly devised myth" by noting his own experience with Christ on the holy Mount of Transfiguration. Then follows, in ch. 1:19-21, Peter's classic reference to the inspiration of Scripture: "And we have the prophetic word made more sure. You will do well to pay attention to this as to a lamp shining in a dark place, until the day dawns and the morning star rises in your hearts. First of all you must understand this, that no prophecy of scripture is a matter of one's own interpretation, because no prophecy ever came by the impulse of man, but men moved by the Holy Spirit spoke from God." The "prophetic word made more sure" is probably a reference to the Messianic passages in the Old Testament that had been confirmed by the life and death of Jesus Christ. Therefore, when Peter advises his readers to pay attention to this prophetic word he is referring to the Old Testament books in their possession. These prophetic utterances which they have in writing are not like the man-made ideas put forth by the false teachers of their day, so Peter claims, because "men moved [literally, "borne"] by the Holy Spirit spoke from God." In other words the extant Old Testament copies are trustworthy and authoritative because the original prophecies were God-given. There is no explicit indication in this passage that Peter made any *essential* distinction between the originals and the copies. The important teaching is that the Scriptures had their origin in God; therefore the copies that Peter's readers had were also to be considered as being from God and thus worthy of their careful study.

Neither in these key passages by Paul, Jesus, and Peter nor in the rest of the New Testament passages that refer to the inspiration of the Old Testament are there any explicit statements that single out the autographs as being different in kind from copies. The reason is clearly seen from the New Testament as a whole. In proclaiming and defending the "good news," Jesus and the apostles took as their authority the available manuscripts of the Old Testament books. Their Jewish opponents shared this belief, and so the spiritual battle was waged and won on the common ground of the extant copies of Scripture, not on an abstract reference to the autographs.

Theological Value of the Autographs

Notwithstanding the lack of explicit Biblical teaching about the autographs, the subject came to have an increasingly prominent place in any discussion on inspiration. The earliest non-Biblical formulations of inspiration were general statements that conceived of Scripture as the trustworthy, authoritative Word of God. Implied in trustworthiness, of course, were the aspects of truthfulness and accuracy of the record because the ancients concurred in Balaam's answer to Balak, "God is not man, that he should lie" (Num. 23:19). For the most part, however, this concept of accuracy was applied to the available copies of Scripture. Difficulties in the text were overcome by the allegorical method of interpretation that disregarded the literal meaning of the text and looked for the hidden meaning.

When it became clear to lovers of Scripture that copies of the Hebrew Old Testament and the Greek New Testament contained some errors, it was quite natural to transfer the quality of accuracy or inerrancy to the original writings. Obviously one reason for this new emphasis was to protect the honor and perfection of God. The basis for this assumption was the syllogism: God is perfect, God revealed himself in the autographs, therefore the autographs had to be inerrant. A closely related reason for this doctrine was to guarantee the value and the authority of extant Bibles. According to this argument, without the presupposition of a perfect original text one could just as well turn to Buddhist or Hindu literature.[2] In brief, even though our Bibles are an approximation of the original manuscripts, their value and authority are ensured, so it is claimed, by the assumption of inerrant autographs.

The desire to honor God and to contend for the uniqueness of his revelation is indeed praiseworthy, but the question is whether the assumptions back of the syllogism are in accord with the facts. In other words, do the events of redemptive history reveal the kind of God presupposed by the deduction inherent in the doctrine of inerrant autographs?

Each autograph of a Biblical book (coming at irregular intervals over many centuries) served as a standard of reference for only a short time—an exceedingly short time, considering the span of the Judeo-Christian religion. Aside from the few manuscripts copied from the original documents, the autographs had little standardizing control because they soon perished, either through continual use or because of deterioration.

Thus, for centuries before the church came into existence, and for a century after, the Old Testament books were transmitted with no standard text being employed to gauge the accuracy of copies. Yet, in spite of this fact, God's kingdom grew and spread worldwide. Actually, for more than 99 percent of the people involved in the Judeo-Christian tradition, knowledge of God has come through copies of Scripture, none of which was inerrant. In short, errant copies of Biblical books have not hindered the Holy Spirit in his convicting and illuminating activities.

On the other hand, when the role of Scripture is directed toward specific issues of faith and practice, there is a valid basis in appealing to the autographs. For example, persons who justify religious snake-handling on the authority of Mark 16:18 need to know that the last twelve verses of our copies of Mark are not the original conclusion to that Gospel account. It is right and reasonable, therefore, to ascertain as nearly as possible the text of the original manuscripts. Only insofar as the accidents of transmission are removed can one be sure what was originally written. It was primarily in relation to faith and practice that traditional formulations of inspiration ascribed infallibility to Scripture, but inasmuch as all of Scripture does not pertain to faith and practice the task of textual criticism is not necessarily grounded in the assumption of inerrancy. Moreover, since God has seen fit to work through errant copies of Scripture, is one justified in claiming that God *had* to give the autographs inerrantly?

It is very instructive to observe how much stress those who believe in the doctrine of inerrant autographs put on the trustworthiness of our present Hebrew and Greek texts. One representative scholar says of Scripture: "We may truly say that by God's peculiar providence it has been preserved free from serious error. We may say that to all intents and purposes we have the words that prophets and apostles wrote — and this was nothing less than the verbally inspired Word of the living God." [3] If extant texts "free from serious error" are authoritative enough to be considered, "to all intents and purposes," the words of the prophets and the apostles, then is it not valid to acknowledge that the autographs also had some inconsequential errors and were to all intents and purposes the pure, authoritative Word of God? Is it actually true that some defects in the autographs would have reduced Scripture to the level of Hindu or Buddhist sacred literature?

Why Did the Autographs Perish?

The question still remains as to why God permitted the autographs to perish or be lost. These documents, some have suggested, would have become more revered with the passing of time and possibly even worshiped as was the bronze serpent that Moses made. Others see benefit in the loss of the autographs because it removes any necessity of determining which of our extant manuscripts are copies and which are original. This also removes the further possibility of some person's claiming autograph status for a manuscript with erroneous teachings.

We can be sure that if we had the autographs some persons would revere or even worship them, and still others would doubt their authenticity, but in neither case does the suggestion get at the heart of the problem. The important thing about the autographs is, after all, not the manuscript itself but the assumed inerrancy of the document. If God, through his Spirit, could have given the original writings inerrantly, then he surely could have enabled the scribes to copy the autograph of each of the Old Testament books without a mistake, maintaining in the copy thereby the precise accuracy of the original manuscript. This process of transmission could have been carried on quite apart from the fate of the autographs once one copy had been made. The real problem, therefore, is not why God let the autographs perish, but why God did not maintain in the copies of Scripture the assumed inerrancy of the original manuscripts.

One proposal in this connection suggests that maybe the benefit reaped during the last century and a half from all the textual, linguistic, and archaeological studies is the reason why God did not transmit the Scriptures inerrantly.[4] But how did errant copies of Scripture benefit those who lived prior to A.D. 1800 or thereabouts?

In the final analysis, is it necessary to attribute reasons to God for the loss of the autographs or the failure to transmit Scripture inerrantly? God did not have to set forth any *special* purpose with respect to the fate of the original manuscripts. He knew what would happen to them in the natural order of wear and decay. What is plain, however, is that God did not purpose to maintain in transmission the accuracy of the autographs. He could allow his revelation to flow through human channels, for he knew that the accuracy of certain human minds devoted to him would be sufficient to maintain the level of truth necessary for achieving his purposes.

3: *Transmission, Translation, and Inspiration*

TRANSMISSION of Biblical material has many more implications for the doctrine of inspiration than the few noted in the previous chapter. It is generally acknowledged that any extended bit of scribal activity results in some kind of error. The Book of Jeremiah, as we have observed, was compiled over a number of years with units being added after the completion of the second scroll in 604 B.C. Even if one considers this document to have been inerrant, is one warranted in claiming that in all the scribal activity of copying and inserting the new material the compiler was inerrant? If the facts necessitate the redefining of " autograph " in terms of an anthology or collection, then is it not imperative that the doctrine of inerrancy cover all phases of that complex process as well? So it would seem. Let us turn to the Biblical data, therefore, to see whether this conclusion is valid.

Transmission of Source Material

An excellent example of the difficulty that *process* poses is the historical account presented in Chronicles as compared with that in Samuel-Kings. As a general rule, the figures in Chronicles are larger than the corresponding figures of the parallel accounts in Samuel-Kings. In II Sam. 24:9, Joab reports 800,000 " valiant men who drew the sword " available in Israel, and 500,000 in Judah. I Chronicles 21:5 has 1,100,000 men in Israel, and 470,000 in Judah. The latter statistic is an example of some instances in which

Chronicles has the smaller figure, but this is the exception. II Chronicles 13:17 speaks of 500,000 " picked men " of Israel being slain by Judah, and in II Chron. 14:9, 13 report that Zerah the Ethiopian came up against Judah with 1,000,000 men, none of whom remained alive.

If, as some believe, the Hebrew expression " thousand thousands " means a vast army rather than precisely a million men, then one wonders why I Chron. 21:5 adds 100,000 to the supposedly round number represented by 1,000,000. Furthermore, the other reference to 470,000 is hardly intended as a round number. Another method of accounting for the excessive figures is to consider them as scribal mistakes in the transmission of the books of Chronicles. Errors of this kind would tend to level out, however, and occur as frequently in Samuel-Kings as in Chronicles. Evidently the large numbers must be accounted for in still another manner.

The available data indicate that II Kings was not complete until about 560 B.C. (the thirty-seventh year of the captivity of Jehoiachin, noted in II Kings 25:27). If, as William F. Albright and tradition contend, the Chronicler was Ezra, then the books of Chronicles would date from around 425 B.C. While Ezra employed some sources that were overlooked by, or not known to, the compiler of Samuel-Kings, the bulk of the material concerning Judah, the Southern Kingdom, was common to both histories.

There was at least one significant difference, however. Ezra's sources had acquired the enlarged figures during the period of transmission since the compilation of II Kings. It is a well-known fact that numbers in inscriptions of the Assyrian kings, for example, tended to increase with each new edition of the annals. This was due partly to the human tendency to magnify gradually the glories of the past as time widens the gap. Some of the enlarged figures were no doubt accidental errors of the scribes because numbers were indicated, more often than not, by a series of marks or tallies instead of being spelled out. Possibly both of these tendencies helped to account for the exaggerated numbers, but regardless of how they came to be, they probably appeared in the original manuscripts of Chronicles.

After I Chron. 8:32, in his renowned commentary on the Bible, Matthew Henry acknowledges quite frankly: "As to the difficulties that occur in this and the foregoing genealogies we need not perplex ourselves. I presume Ezra took them as he found them *in the books of the kings of Israel and Judah* (ch. ix.1), according as they were given in by the several tribes, each observing what method they thought fit. Hence some ascend, others descend; some have *numbers* affixed, others *places;* some have historical remarks intermixed, others have not; some are shorter, others longer; some agree with other records, others differ; some, it is likely, were torn, erased, and blotted, others more legible. Those of Dan and Reuben were entirely lost. This holy man wrote as he was moved by the Holy Ghost; but there was no necessity for the making up of the defects, no, nor for the rectifying of the mistakes, of these genealogies by inspiration."[1] Thus Henry, the saintly student of Scripture, felt quite free to admit that the autograph of Chronicles was mistaken in some of its details.

Other evangelical scholars have preferred, however, to seek the solution to the difficulty in the providence of God. According to this view the Biblical writers were providentially conditioned men, both by birth and education. Knowledge was conveyed to them by supernatural and natural means. Natural knowledge came through the intuitions, observations, and thought processes of their own experiences, but it also came through sources, both oral and written. These sources were under the general providence of God, so that there was no conflict between the natural knowledge and the supernatural knowledge.[2]

But if this were true, then one of two means had to be employed to ensure the inerrancy of the original Biblical scroll: either God's providence guaranteed the inerrant transmission of the source material or the Spirit of God warned the writer of the mistakes in his sources and then supplied the correct data. There is no Biblical support for either of these theoretical possibilities, and it would appear that Matthew Henry chose the better course in coming to grips with the data of Scripture. This happier solution was also suggested by James Orr (1844–1913): "Where sources of information fail, or where, as may sometimes happen, there are lacunae [omissions], or blots, or misreadings of names, or errors of transcription, such as are incidental to the transmission of all MSS. [manuscripts], it is not to be supposed that supernatural information is granted to supply the lack. Where this is frankly acknowledged, inspiration is cleared from a great many of the difficulties which misapprehension has attached to it." [3]

Transmission of Biblical Manuscripts

The recognition of scribal errors in manuscripts of the Hebrew Old Testament and the Greek New Testament raises the question as to whether God's honor and veracity are really protected by contending for inerrant autographs when one has to turn around immediately and admit that God could not, or did not care to, keep the text inerrant in transmission. After all, if God bore the prophets and apostles along inerrantly in the autographs, then why should it be unthinkable that God could bear up the scribes in such a way that their copies would have the same accuracy as the original manuscripts? In either case God is working through human instrumentality and there is no *inherent* reason why he should have any more difficulty performing the latter feat than the former.

Some evangelicals sense the implications of this apparent inconsistency and so they contend for a God-protected text.[4] But this way out of the difficulty is also inconsistent because one must finally admit that none of our present manuscripts is a perfect reproduction of the autograph. The theory of a God-protected text, therefore, must answer the question, how much imperfection of the text will inerrancy permit?

A good example of the attempt to reconcile copies with autographs is found in the writings of the seventeenth-century theologians. The Lutheran dogmatician D. Hollaz (1648–1713) contended that the apographs (a technical term from Greek, meaning "copies" of Scripture) were the very words and content of the autographs. Writing in a similar vein, J. A. Quenstedt (1617–1688) reasoned: "Every holy Scripture which existed at the time of Paul was *theopneustos* (II Tim. 3:16) and authentic. Not the autographic (for they had perished long before), but the apographic writings existed at the time of Paul. Therefore, the apographic Scripture also is *theopneustos* and authentic. God, not the hand of Moses, gave authenticity to the Pentateuch. For although inspiration and divine authority inhered originally in the autographa [that is, the autographs], these attributes belong to the apographa by virtue of their derivation, since they were faithfully transcribed from them so that not only the sense but also the words were precisely the same." [5] In theory, therefore, Quenstedt is assuming exact transmission of the Old Testament books from their origin down to Paul's time, but it is doubtful that he would go much beyond this period. As Robert Preus comments: "There is certainly no reason to doubt that he, like Hollaz, was aware of the fact of variant readings among the manuscripts then accessible. He would hardly have considered the apographa of his time in the same category as those which Paul and Timothy used. However, this statement indicates that he is not alive to the significance of the fact of variant readings." [6]

From the Dead Sea scrolls we have learned that the text of the standard Hebrew Old Testament available today is much the same as it was in the time of Paul and Timothy. Thus, whether Quenstedt thought so or not, the Hebrew apographs of his day were essentially the same as Paul's, and therefore what could be said of Paul's apographa could also be said of Quenstedt's.

The remarkable fact is Quenstedt's recognition that *theopneustos* in II Tim. 3:16 referred to the apographs of Paul's time. Most likely this objectivity with respect to the Biblical statement resulted from his failure to recognize the significance of textual variants. The oversight permitted him to take Paul literally while still holding to the assumption of inerrant autographs. All he had to do was claim that the words of Paul's apographs were precisely the same as the autographs.

But for some years now, evangelicals have been "alive" to the significance of textual variants and so they have not been able to accept Quenstedt's easy answer. Knowing that any extended bit of scribal activity results in errors, they have admitted, for the most part, that all *copies* of the Old Testament were errant to some degree.

This implication received partial confirmation in 1947 and the subsequent years by the discovery of the Dead Sea scrolls. The Biblical books among the scrolls, dating from the second and first centuries B.C., exhibit a number of scribal errors. Without doubt this condition prevailed in the manuscripts of the first century A.D. as well. Nevertheless, when the Sadducees tried to trick Jesus with a question, he answered them (Mark 12:24), "Is not this why you are wrong, that you know neither the scriptures nor the power of God?" Here, as in John 10:35, Jesus was grounding his appeal in the copies of the Old Testament extant then.

If Jesus and Paul and Peter considered the errant manuscripts of their time as trustworthy and authoritative, should we not have the same attitude toward our manuscripts today? On the basis of II Peter 1:21 some evangelicals contend that there is a very important distinction between the autographs and copies. If "men moved [literally, "borne"] by the Holy Spirit spoke from God," then only what was given at the moment of the Spirit's aid can really be inspired. Because Scripture does not state specifically that scribes and copyists were borne along by the Holy Spirit, one is not warranted, so it is claimed, in maintaining that copies are also inspired.[7]

Obviously, the scribes who made copies of Biblical books were not inspired in the unique sense in which the prophets and the apostles were, but does this fact prevent copies from having the results of God's revelation to the inspired authors? The way in which Jesus, Peter, John, and Paul handle passages derived from their Old Testament copies implies that they considered these copies as preserving both the results of inspiration and the authority that characterized the autographs.

Nowhere does the Bible teach that copies of Scripture are not inspired. What, then, is the basis for this concept? Evidently it stems from an assumption that equates inspiration with inerrancy. This deductive approach to the matter assumes, as we have seen, that God had to reveal himself inerrantly. When the sacred writers were borne along inerrantly by the Holy Spirit their words were truly inspired. Once this assumption is granted, it is clear that scribal errors automatically eliminate copies from the category of inspired literature. But the question still remains, What is the Biblical support for this teaching? Can one really claim Biblical authority for this view when it is in the theological and philosophical discussion which normally follows the treatment of the Biblical passages that the idea of the autographs is brought in?

The teachings and the data of Scripture indicate that the New Testament writers considered the errant manuscripts of the first century A.D. as inspired (that is, containing the results of God's revelation to the inspired Old Testament authors), trustworthy, and authoritative. The extent to which they understood the implications of scribal errors and variant readings is not important. The extant Scriptures had been opened to them by the life and teaching of Jesus, and also the Holy Spirit, working through these errant manuscripts, had wrought a marvelous change in their lives. It is little wonder, then, that from a practical, popular point of view they considered the Scriptures as the very message of God to them. They were not concerned about the autographs as such, nor were they exercised over the difficulties in transmitting the original text. What really mattered was the "here and now"—the reality and power of the Old Testament copies which they had. Are we not justified, therefore, in considering the errant copies of our day, both Old and New Testaments, as inspired, trustworthy, and authoritative?

Translation and Inspiration

A step removed from the problem of manuscript transmission is the issue of translation into another language. Scholars, regardless of their theological views, accept the fact that all translations err in some measure because no one language has terms that correspond exactly to similar terms in another language.[8] Differences of opinion arise when inferences are made from this sound premise. If inerrancy is assumed, the logical inference is that no translation, not even the Septuagint, can be inspired. But again the question is whether this assumption is supported by evidence from the New Testament and contemporary sources.

Origin of the Septuagint

While the story of the Septuagint's origin (recorded in the letter of Aristeas to Philocrates) has been proved to be a late, fanciful explanation, some features are of importance. This story says that the idea of translating the Hebrew Pentateuch into Greek came from Demetrius, the librarian at Alexandria, Egypt. He proposed it to the king, Ptolemy II (Philadelphus), who reigned 285–247 B.C. The suggestion met with approval and Ptolemy sent a letter to Eleazar, high priest at Jerusalem, requesting seventy-two elders (six from each of the twelve tribes) known for their exemplary life, knowledge of the law, and ability to translate.

The request was granted, and the Jewish scholars went to Alexandria, where they were given a royal reception by the king himself. Seven banquets were held for them, all of which observed strictly the dietary laws of the Jews. To avoid the distractions and oppressive conditions of the city, the translators were taken to the island of Pharos in the harbor of Alexandria. Here in magnificent surroundings with everything provided for their convenience, the translators set to work. The account in the letter relates: "And so they proceeded to carry it out, making all details harmonize by mutual comparisons. The appropriate result of the harmonization was reduced to writing under the direction of Demetrius." [9] After explaining some of the daily routine, the letter states, "And so it came about that the work of transcription was completed in seventy-two days, as if this coincidence had been the result of some design." [10] Whatever the historical basis for this story, it shows that the Alexandrian Jews considered the Septuagint as the product of God's providence, given by inspiration.

Most certainly Philo knew something of this tradition (although he shows ignorance of the letter of Aristeas to Philocrates) because his account of the Septuagint's origin has certain features of the story in expanded form. He believed, for example, that the translators "under inspiration, wrote, not each several scribe something different, but the same word for word, as though dictated to each by an invisible prompter." [11] There was no need to harmonize the seventy-two translations because all of them agreed word for word. This was an even greater coincidence than that of completing the translation in exactly seventy-two days.

In trying to support the authenticity of this marvelous feat, Philo proceeds to explain: "Yet who does not know that every language, and Greek especially, abounds in terms, and that the same thought can be put in many shapes by changing single words and whole phrases and suiting the expression to the occasion? This was not the case, we are told, with this law of ours, but the Greek words used corresponded literally with the Chaldean [Hebrew], exactly suited to the things they indicated. For, just as in geometry and logic, so it seems to me, the sense indicated does not admit of variety in the expression which remains unchanged in its original form, so these writers, as it clearly appears, arrived at a wording which corresponded with the matter, and alone, or better than any other, would bring out clearly what was meant. The clearest proof of this is that, if Chaldeans have learned Greek, or Greeks Chaldean, and read both versions, the Chaldean and the translation, they regard them with awe and reverence as sisters, or rather one and the same, both in matter and words, and speak of the authors not as translators but as prophets and priests of the mysteries, whose sincerity and singleness of thought has enabled them to go hand in hand with the purest of spirits, the spirit of Moses."[12] For Philo, then, the Septuagint was as divinely inspired and authoritative as the Hebrew Scriptures because the translators were endued with such a measure of God's Spirit that they were in the category of the prophets and the priests, even the greatest prophet, Moses. Philo spanned the first centuries B.C. and A.D., and there is every reason to believe that his views represent those commonly held by the Jews of that time.

New Testament and the Septuagint

Jesus, the apostles (including Paul), and other leaders who helped found the church were Jews. Did they share Philo's view of the Septuagint? New Testament evidence points in this direction. More than half of the quotations from the Old Testament are from the Septuagint rather than being the New Testament writer's own translation of the Hebrew text into Greek. The book of Hebrews quotes extensively, and invariably the source is the Septuagint. Many of the quotations in Paul's letters are also derived from the Septuagint.

In fact, the arguments of the New Testament writers often hinge on the reading in the Septuagint. In Heb. 10:5-9, for example, the author is talking about the "offering of the body of Jesus Christ once for all." Into Jesus' mouth are placed the words of Ps. 40:6-8, the heart of the quotation from the Septuagint being "a body hast thou prepared for me." But the corresponding line in the Hebrew text reads, literally, "Ears thou hast dug for me," meaning, "Thou hast given me an open ear." Yet this meaning (while somewhat related to the meaning in the Septuagint) was not the precise idea which the author of Hebrews had in mind. His key word in the unit in ch. 10 is "body," and because this word occurs in the Septuagint passage he makes use of the quotation.

Moreover, the inference " translation = no inspiration " poses a real problem in the Gospels. Probably most of what Jesus said in public and to his disciples was in Aramaic. But the *inspired original Gospels were written in Greek;* that is, the *autographs* of the Gospels *were translations* for the most part. Consistency would mean denying the Gospels the rank of inspired Scripture, but no one has dared follow the inference to its ultimate conclusion.

Under the pressure of accounting for different words in the Gospels, some evangelicals are quite eager to explain them as differences in translation of the original Aramaic statement back of the Greek autographs. As a corollary of this argument, they affirm that translation does not impair the original teaching. It is even recognized by some that the Christian church would not suffer unduly should all the Hebrew manuscripts perish and only the Septuagint remain.[13] Yet having made these very accurate and valid statements, these same persons are constrained to deny inspiration to any translation. The apparent reason for this conclusion is the inference that since all translations err, no translation can be inspired. Here, as in the case of manuscript transmission, inspiration is tied to inerrancy.

As observed previously, there is a sense in which the autographs can be distinguished from copies of the original records. The uniquely inspired servant of God is involved with the autograph, whereas the scribe who produces copies has only that degree of inspiration common to all devoted men of God. When viewed solely as written records, however, there is no reason, aside from the doctrine of inerrancy, to distinguish a copy from the autograph. As long as the copy has the essential results of God's revelation to the prophet or apostle, one is warranted in considering the copy as truly inspired as the autograph. This seems to have been the view of Jesus and the New Testament writers.

The next question is whether they held the same respect for the Septuagint. We have already observed that Paul's use of *theopneustos* in II Tim. 3:16 applies to the manuscript copies of his day. In v. 15 Paul refers to " the sacred writings " with which Timothy has been acquainted from his childhood. But what were these writings? The Hebrew, or the Septuagint, or both?

Timothy lived in Derbe or Lystra in Asia Minor. His father was a Greek and his mother a Jewess (Acts 16:1). He received his spiritual heritage and training from his grandmother Lois and his mother Eunice (II Tim. 1:5). When Paul wanted Timothy to accompany him " he took him and circumcised him because of the Jews that were in those places, for they all knew that his father was a Greek " (Acts 16:3). This information along with the popularity of the Septuagint among the Jews of the Dispersion (such as in Asia Minor) and the widespread belief in its inspiration make a very strong case for the Septuagint as "the sacred writings" in Timothy's religious experience.

There is no evidence to show that the apostles denied the inspiration of the LXX. On the contrary, the extent and manner of its use in the New Testament imply a high regard for it not unlike the view held by Philo. Were the apostles to return now, they would likely be amazed to learn that, according to some Biblical scholars, they did not believe in the inspiration of the Septuagint. The apostolic respect for the LXX was carried on in the early church and we find such theological giants as Irenaeus and Augustine championing the view.

Since Augustine's mother tongue was Latin, he read as his Bible the Old Latin translation, the extant copies of which swarmed with scribal mistakes. Thus, in a letter to Jerome, he comments: " If I do find anything in those [canonical] books which seems contrary to truth, I decide that either the text is corrupt, or the translator did not follow what was really said, or that I failed to understand it. . . . I do not believe that you want your books to be read as if they were those of prophets or apostles, about whose writings, free of all error, it is unlawful to doubt." [14]

This affirmation has been commonly interpreted to be a clear reference to the inerrancy of the original writings of Scripture, but with respect to the Old Testament it contends rather for the inerrancy of the Septuagint. This is made quite clear in another context where Augustine declares: "In emending any Latin translations, we must consult the Greek texts; of these, the reputation of the seventy translators [that is, the Septuagint] is most distinguished in regard to the Old Testament. . . . Who, then, would venture to put anything on a level with this authority; still less, esteem anything better? . . . Therefore, even if we discover something in the Hebrew original other than they have interpreted it, it is my opinion that we should yield to the divine direction."[15] Thus, the wording of the manuscripts of the Septuagint extant in Augustine's day was to be preferred over the wording of the available Hebrew manuscripts. In this context it is clear that Augustine's designation "Hebrew original" means the extant Hebrew manuscripts, and, accordingly, the term "original" refers to the original language in which the Old Testament books were written, not to the original writings (autographs). Furthermore, Augustine made no specific reference to the original copy of the Septuagint. He assumed, along with Philo, the New Testament writers, and Irenaeus, that the authority of the Septuagint rested in the wording of the available manuscripts.

A very sane evaluation of the situation was made by the translators of the King James Version. In the preface, "The Translators to the Reader," they comment concerning the Septuagint: "It is certain, that that translation was not so sound and so perfect, but that it needed in many places correction; and who had been so sufficient for this work as the apostles or apostolic men? Yet it seemed good to the Holy Ghost and to them, to take that which they found, (the same being for the greatest part true and sufficient) rather than by making a new, in that new world and green age of the church, to expose themselves to many exceptions and cavillations, as though they made a translation to serve their own turn, and therefore bearing witness to themselves, their witness not to be regarded." The King James translators, unlike Philo, recognized mistakes in the Septuagint, yet they believed in its sufficiency. They were also wise enough to see that if God had wanted the apostles to make their own Greek translation of the Hebrew, he would have set them to the task. Rather, a new translation would have posed a problem, because the Jews would have continually accused the Christians of reading their own ideas into the translation. As it was, the Septuagint had been translated by Jews long before the coming of Christ and the Christian church, and so it could serve as the common ground of appeal. If in God's sight the Septuagint was not really inspired, then why did it seem good to the Holy Spirit and the apostles to use it? This is the crucial question. If the facts account for anything, they show that God rejects the inference that translations cannot be inspired because they have some errors. The correct inference, therefore, is that in spite of some mistakes, all reasonably accurate translations of Scripture are inspired.

How far can one take this principle? Only God can say. In some cases translations have been pitifully weak because the earnestness of the missionary translator was not matched with a corresponding facility in the native language of the translation. But in spite of errors scattered throughout these translations, enough of the truth was retained to bring the readers under the convicting power of the Holy Spirit. As a result, lives were transformed and whole churches came into being. When one observes God working his purpose through such imperfect means, has one the right to exclude such a translation from the category of inspired writings?

4: *Inerrancy and the Phenomena of Scripture*

THE DISCUSSION thus far has dealt with Biblical teachings and data that are instructive with respect to the autographs, manuscript transmission, and translations. This evidence, when viewed inductively, seems to indicate that the Bible makes no essential distinction between the three categories of Scripture. All three are considered as trustworthy and authoritative because they derive ultimately from God. However, the Biblical writers did not express themselves on many technical aspects related to the doctrine of inspiration; therefore there is the genuine problem of trying to determine just how far implications and areas of silence can be elaborated and still be true to the intent of the writers. Those who approach the issue deductively with the assumption that God, if he were truly God, had to reveal himself inerrantly are inclined to see this teaching as a clear implication of the Biblical passages.

Both approaches are sincere, but both can hardly be correct in the areas where they come to opposite conclusions. In the interests of truth, there needs to be some careful consideration of the phenomena or data of Scripture that have relevance for the concept of inerrancy. Let it be said at the outset, however, that it is not the writer's intention to parade the difficulties of Scripture. Those to be considered have been known for many years, but additional information warrants a new discussion of the issues.

Jude 14

Jude says in v. 14 of his one-chapter letter, "It was of these also that Enoch in the seventh generation from Adam prophesied, saying," and then follows a quotation that is found in I Enoch 1:9. The latter is one of a series of Jewish books not included within the Old Testament canon. These were written, for the most part, in the period between the Old and New Testaments. The general term for these noncanonical books is the Greek word *apocrypha* (meaning "hidden," either because they were thought to be too difficult for the common person to understand, or they were considered spurious). But the book of Enoch is usually classified among the *pseudepigrapha* (literally, "false writings") because the author, employing a fictitious name, gives the impression that the work comes from a Biblical character.

The specific problem concerning us here is not, however, the quotation from an apocryphal or pseudepigraphic book. The difficulty lies in Jude's qualifying statement "seventh from Adam." Every known manuscript of Jude has this qualification, so there is good reason to believe that it came from Jude himself. But what did Jude mean by inserting this additional phrase? Some have interpreted the insertion as a literary device identifying the source of Jude's quotation in terms commonly accepted by his readers. According to this view, then, the insertion would not express Jude's actual thoughts as to the ultimate source of the quotation. In brief, "seventh from Adam" is taken as the claim in the book of Enoch: for example, Enoch is reported as saying, "I was born the seventh in the first week, while judgment and righteousness still endured" (I Enoch 93:3), and Noah, the grandson of Enoch, purports to mention "the garden where the elect and righteous dwell, where my grandfather was taken up, the seventh from Adam, the first man whom the Lord of Spirits created" (I Enoch 60:8). These references to "seventh" stem from the genealogical table found in Gen. ch. 5.

On the other hand, Jude quotes I Enoch 1:9 as a *prophecy*

which is being fulfilled in his day. Would he have done so had he thought the book and the passage originated during the period between the Testaments? Does not the cruciality of the quotation indicate, rather, that Jude thought the authority of his source derived from Enoch, the pre-Flood patriarch, who was taken up by God when he was 365 years old? At least for many centuries this was the traditional interpretation of Jude's intent. When the book of Enoch came to light, tradition generally solved the problem by claiming that Jude's source was oral tradition and that Enoch was a later book which copied from Jude.

This attempt at solving the difficulty has proved to be baseless, however. Portions of various copies of Enoch have been found among the Dead Sea (Qumrân) scrolls. These date mainly from the first century B.C., so without question Jude got his quotation from a copy of the book of Enoch. There is good evidence (for example, the defense of a solar calendar) to show that the Enoch literature originated within the Qumrân (Essene) tradition. Mainstream Judaism, on the contrary, followed a lunar calendar, consequently the book of Enoch was considered heretical. Even though the book was not incorporated in the Septuagint, the early Christians (with many affinities to the Qumrân group) accepted it. This is quite evident because the New Testament is influenced more directly by the book of Enoch than by any other noncanonical book. Jude clearly alludes to the book in v. 6 and he quotes it in vs. 14-15, but his apparent conviction that the quotation derived from Enoch the Patriarch is untenable. As Edward Carnell observes, "Of course, orthodoxy can always say that Jude knew by inspiration that the seventh from Adam spoke the words that now appear in the book of Enoch; but the explanation sounds suspiciously affected."[1]

If one is to contend that the book of Enoch represents an oral tradition stemming from the Patriarch, one should also account in similar fashion for the mass of literature that appears in the inter-testament period under the names of various Old Testament characters. It is exceedingly strange that not one reference is made in the Old Testament to any such literature. One reads of the book of Jashar but never the book of Enoch. Is it possible that Abraham, Isaac, Jacob, and the Israelites knew of this oral tradition and yet failed to mention it? Hardly. It is equally difficult to show that God preserved the material by an oral tradition distinct from Abraham and the people of promise.

The facts at hand would seem to indicate that Jude did not realize the origin of his source. However, this view is criticized by some because it is made on partial evidence. Maybe further information would vindicate Jude, so it is reasoned. But an *argument from silence* is recognized by all to be quite weak. It implies that one must have almost total evidence before demonstration is possible. If this is the case, one could argue just as cogently that there may have been airplanes in the time of Christ. By this period, man had conceived of the idea of human flight and he knew how to work metals, etc., so why not airplanes? While this proposition sounds fantastic, it would be difficult to produce sufficient data to disprove the claim in the mind of the proponent. He could always say that someday the evidence would be forthcoming to prove his point. Likewise, in the case of Jude's quotation from Enoch, absolute proof will probably never be accessible, but is this justification enough for the fond hope of having the problem resolved in favor of Jude?

There is, of course, a place for the argument from silence, but it should not be used unless the available evidence permits a *genuine probability,* not a theoretical possibility, that the proposition is true. In far too many cases the argument from silence is resorted to only when the facts are on the side of one's opponents. On the contrary, it is amazing how little evidence it usually takes to convince a person of a point when it agrees with his presuppositions. To some extent every human being is guilty of wishful thinking, but there must come a time when the facts become determinative, and in the case of inerrancy Jude 14 is as good a place to start as any.

Either the quotation originated with Enoch the Patriarch or it did not. Aside from Jude's claim, all the evidence indicates that it did not. Jude did not intend to deceive or falsify the issue. His error was an innocent one which he made in common with his fellow Jews and Christians. But sincerity of motive did not eliminate the mistake. Moreover, the Holy Spirit did not override the human concept of Jude. How, then, does this accord with the dogma that the Holy Spirit " bore " the writers along, guiding them inerrantly in all that they wrote? The seriousness of the problem is also indicated by the fear of many even to recognize the difficulty; for example, commentaries by evangelicals seldom discuss the problem.

Jude 9

The little book of Jude is a warning against false brethren who have infiltrated the Christian ranks and undermined " the faith which was once for all delivered to the saints " (v. 3). Jude reminds his readers that God will punish such sinners, and as proof he cites three examples: the unbelieving Israelites who died in the wilderness (v. 5), the fallen angels chained in nether gloom (v. 6), and the immoral residents of Sodom and Gomorrah who perished by fire (v. 7). The first and last examples are described in the Pentateuch and without question the author considered them as historical events in God's dealing with mankind. Apparently Jude considered God's condemnation of the fallen angels (described in an expansion of Gen. 6:1-4 found in the book of Enoch) as an actual happening in the past.

In contrast to the revilings of the false brethren, " loudmouthed boasters " (v. 16) who " boldly carouse " (v. 12) at love feasts, Jude cites in v. 9 the example of the archangel Michael: " But when the archangel Michael, contending with the devil, disputed about the body of Moses, he did not presume to pronounce a reviling judgment upon him, but said, 'the Lord rebuke you.' "

The event to which Jude alludes is not recorded in the canonical Old Testament. His source was another apocryphal book, The Assumption of Moses, which is usually dated early in the first century A.D. After the death of Moses, according to this account, the archangel Michael had to contend with Satan for the body. Satan claimed the body because Moses had been a murderer (Ex. 2:11). This blasphemous charge was intolerable to Michael, but rather than accuse Satan of blasphemy he simply said, "The Lord rebuke you."

While some have interpreted Jude's allusion to the apocryphal book as an argument *ad hominem* in which he cites the passage because the book was respected by his opponents, one gets the impression, just as in v. 6, that Jude believed the incident was an actual fact and thus a valid basis for refuting his adversaries.

But Jude 9 (which was also a part of the autograph of Jude) is, according to the traditional view, just as much inspired as John 3:16. If it is inspired, then why be hesitant about discussing the implications? Either the archangel Michael contended with the devil for the body of Moses or he did not. Joshua and the prophets never refer to any such struggle, so there is no Biblical reason, aside from Jude's allusion, for believing in the actuality of the story. On the other hand, does not the authoritative function of Jude's illustration show the importance that he attached to it? If, as the evidence seems to indicate, Jude accepted the current tradition with respect to the body of Moses, what becomes of the doctrine of inerrancy?

The Reign of Pekah

According to II Kings 15:27, "in the fifty-second year of Azariah king of Judah Pekah the son of Remaliah began to reign over Israel in Samaria, and reigned twenty years." For some years now, the figure 20 has been known to be wrong. James Orr, speaking of the cross references or synchronisms in the books of Kings, said, "Pekah's twenty years in II Kings 15:27 . . . is shown by the Assyrian synchronisms to be a mistake."[2] He did not explain further, and nothing was generally accessible to the layman until Edwin R. Thiele's *The Mysterious Numbers of the Hebrew Kings* appeared in 1951.

The chronology of the kings of Israel and Judah is one of the most complex problems in all the Bible, but Thiele has given sufficient evidence to clinch the matter concerning Pekah's twenty years. In the ancient world there were two systems for reckoning the years of a king's reign, the difference between the two being a matter of one year. Since Israel followed one system and Judah the other during part of their histories, there is often a difference of one year in the records. To simplify the discussion, both of Pekah's reign and of Hezekiah's reign (which is to follow), a single date will be used in each case, although technically the actual date may be a year off one way or the other. Furthermore, unless indicated otherwise, all references in the two sections will be from II Kings.

The verse in question (ch. 15:27) says Pekah began to reign in the fifty-second year of Azariah (another name for Uzziah). Azariah's death, coming in the fifty-second year of his reign, occurred about 739 B.C., and therefore Pekah's reign began then. This was also the year in which Isaiah the prophet "saw the Lord . . . high and lifted up" (Isa. 6:1). If Pekah is given his twenty years, then he finished in 719. The Biblical record says Hoshea, the last king of Israel, followed Pekah and reigned for nine years. This would mean that Samaria, the capital of Israel, fell in 710. However, archaeological evidence has confirmed beyond doubt that Samaria submitted to the Assyrians in 722. It is impossible, then, to give Pekah his twenty years after 739 B.C.

Accordingly, some early commentators figured back twenty years from 731, the end of Pekah's reign and the beginning of Hoshea's. But this reconstruction is equally impossible. Pekah was preceded by Pekahiah (two years) and Menahem (ten years). If Pekah's reign began in 751, then Menahem reigned from 763–753. Yet ch. 15:19 informs us, "Pul the king of Assyria came against the land; and Menahem gave Pul a thousand talents of silver, that he might help him to confirm his hold of the royal power." "Pul" was the Babylonian nickname for the great Assyrian king Tiglath-pileser III, whose dates (745–727) have also been settled beyond question. The annals of Tiglath-pileser refer to this same event, mentioning Menahem by name. Since the payment of tribute was made in 743 or later, Menahem could not have reigned 763–753. If Menahem cannot be moved Pekahiah's reign must remain, 741–739, with Pekah's rule beginning in 739. Inasmuch as his reign closed in 731, the twenty years ascribed to him shrink to eight.

Some scholars have accounted for Pekah's twenty years by assuming that he began reigning as a rival king in Israel at the same time Menahem did. He may have played a small part in the revolt during which Shallum was slain and Menahem set up his new dynasty (ch. 15:14), but he was in no sense a king because he was a *shalish* "captain, official" under Menahem's son, Pekahiah, the man he slew in order to gain power (ch. 15:25). Thiele is most likely correct in suggesting that Pekah took credit to himself for the twelve years that Menahem and Pekahiah had ruled.[3] Evidently Pekah, the usurper, wanted to blot out the memory of the Menahem dynasty and so he had the records changed to show that the Pekah dynasty began in 751. It is virtually certain, therefore, that the notation of a twenty-year reign for Pekah originated in the court records of Israel.

Most scholars recognize that the twenty years assigned to Pekah are in error, but some are still inclined to account for it as a scribal error in transmission of the text of ch. 15:27. This argument fails to reckon, however, with two synchronisms in ch. 15:32 and ch. 16:1. The text of ch. 15:32 notes that Jotham began to reign in "the second year of Pekah." Jotham began to reign as a coregent with his father Uzziah (who was a leper, II Chron. 26:21) about 750. If this date was considered the second year of Pekah, then his first year would have been 751. In other words, the scribe who compiled this section had assigned 751–731 as the time of Pekah's reign. The most plausible explanation for the scribe's action is that his records also attributed a twenty-year reign to Pekah. He was working up his synchronisms between the kings of Israel and of Judah about 125 to 150 years after the fall of Samaria, and so he had no way to check the accuracy of the data that had come from the Northern Kingdom. In making his comparative chart, he gave Pekah twenty years, not realizing that it was impossible (as we have noted) to put

Menahem's reign 763–753 and Pekahiah's 753–751. This slip may appear a bit foolish, but the scribe in Judah knew nothing of B.C. or A.D. and the specific numbers we are using as dates. He did not have an absolute time scale (with Tiglath-pileser's dates, for example) to warn him that he could not actually give Pekah twenty years.

In ch. 16:1 the scribe notes that Ahaz began to reign in "the seventeenth year of Pekah." This synchronism is obviously based on the assumption that Pekah reigned twenty years. But the interesting fact is that once we grant the original error of twenty years instead of eight, the dates which this relative chart gives for Jotham (750) and Ahaz (735) prove to be amazingly accurate. On the other hand, if the original text of II Kings had been inerrant (that is, in accord with the actual reigns of Menahem, 751–741, and of Pekah, 739–731), the scribe would have had Jotham beginning in "the second year of Menahem" and Ahaz starting in "the fifth year of Pekah."

Some of those who contend for the doctrine of an inerrant original text take the next logical step by suggesting that the synchronisms are later scribal insertions that did not appear in the original text of II Kings. But again the suggestion is fruitless. Chapter 15:33 begins, "He was twenty-five years old when he began to reign, and he reigned sixteen years in Jerusalem." If ch. 15:32 is dropped, then "he" refers back to Pekah, who is discussed in ch. 15:31. This is impossible, however, so there is no other way out but to admit that the erroneous details of chs. 15:27, 32; 16:1 were in the original compilation of II Kings.

The Reign of Hezekiah

Another difficult chronological problem has to do with the dates of Hezekiah's reign. Chapter 18:1 states, "In the third year of Hoshea son of Elah, king of Israel, Hezekiah the son of Ahaz, king of Judah, began to reign." Hoshea began reigning in 731, when he slew Pekah (ch. 15:30). According to ch. 18:1, then, Hezekiah began to reign about 728. But ch. 18:13 notes that Sennacherib invaded Judah in "the fourteenth year of King Hezekiah." Since Sennacherib's campaign against Judah and Jerusalem was in 701, Hezekiah began his reign in 715. He ruled for twenty-nine years (ch. 18:2), that is, down to 686. This conclusion is also in line with the inference from ch. 20:6 that after Hezekiah's illness (which occurred about the time of Sennacherib's campaign) God spared his life fifteen years. Practically all scholars are agreed now that Hezekiah reigned 715–686. Then what is to be done with ch. 18:1, which seems to begin Hezekiah's reign in 728?

In discussing this problem, Thiele writes, "Long after the original records of the kings had been set in order and when the true arrangement of the reigns had been forgotten — certain synchronisms in II Kings, chs. 17 and 18, were introduced by some late hand strangely out of harmony with the original pattern of reigns."[4] In Thiele's opinion, some scribe gave Pekah his twenty years, but this time the reign was started at 739 and pushed down twenty years. Thus Hoshea's reign was 719–710. On the basis of this chart, the scribe noted that it was in the third year of Hoshea, about 716, that Hezekiah began to reign. With this interpretation both ch. 18:1 and ch. 18:13 indicate the same time (716–715) for the start of Hezekiah's reign.

Chapter 17:1 indicates that Hoshea began to reign in "the twelfth year of Ahaz." Ahaz' reign of sixteen years (ch. 16:2) began in 731, therefore his twelfth year was 719, the year (according to the scribe's chart) that Hoshea began to rule. The scribe went farther and noted in ch. 18:9-10 that the siege of Samaria began in Hezekiah's fourth year and ended in his sixth. Thus, in Thiele's judgment, the synchronisms in chs. 17:1; 18:1, 9-10 are erroneous because the scribe allotted Pekah twenty years, 739–719.

In the joint article, "Chronology of the Old Testament," pages 212–223, in *The New Bible Dictionary,* K. A. Kitchen and T. C. Mitchell state that Thiele's interpretation of the four synchronisms is invalid. They feel that "the twelfth year" noted in ch. 17:1 refers to Ahaz' last year of a twelve-year coregency with

Jotham, rather than to the twelfth year of his sole reign. Hoshea began in 731, so according to this assumption Ahaz became a coregent with his father Jotham in 743. Chapter 16:2 ascribes to Ahaz a sixteen-year reign (undoubtedly the period 731–715), but the previous verse (ch. 16:1) tells us that his reign began in 735. Mitchell and Kitchen interpret this to mean that Ahaz became a "senior partner" at that time. It is even more probable that the pro-Assyrian group in Judah forced Jotham (who, like his father Uzziah, was anti-Assyrian) to relinquish the rule to his son Ahaz. The policy of Ahaz was decidedly pro-Assyrian (II Chron. 28:16) and it was he, not Jotham, who was the active king when Rezin and Pekah came up (about 734) against Jerusalem (Isa. 7:1). Ahaz was twenty when he began to reign (ch. 16:2), but the text does not make it clear which beginning (735 or 731) was intended. If the former date was meant, then Ahaz was twelve years old in 743; otherwise he was eight. In 751, when he began his twelve-year coregency with Uzziah, Jotham was twenty-five (ch. 15:33). The question is whether in fact Ahaz began a twelve-year coregency in 743 when he was only twelve (or possibly eight) and when Jotham, his father, was himself technically a coregent (because Uzziah did not die until 739).

To account for ch. 18:1, 9-10, Kitchen and Mitchell have also to postulate a twelve-year coregency for Hezekiah (beginning about 728, when he was thirteen years old). In other words, their solution necessitates twelve-year coregencies for three successive kings: Jotham, Ahaz, and Hezekiah. This coincidence does not rule out the possibility, but it raises some doubt. Clearly, the interpretation of the synchronisms in II Kings, chs. 17 and 18, hinges on the number 12. Did Ahaz and Hezekiah, like Jotham, have twelve-year coregencies (making the synchronisms technically accurate) or was Pekah given twelve years beyond his actual reign (thus resulting in erroneous synchronisms). It is difficult to prove which view is correct, but in any case the final solution does not alter the fact of the erroneous details in II Kings 15:27, 32; 16:1.

In discussing the problem of inerrant autographs — the "infallible Bible-X," as he puts it — Emil Brunner comments: "Thus an otherwise absolutely honorable orthodox view of the authority of the Bible was forced to descend to apologetic artifices of this kind. As a result the theology of the church became, and rightly, the butt of scientific criticism. In the long run this solution was untenable. At present it only continues to drag out an unhappy existence in certain Fundamentalist circles." [5] This often-quoted criticism has been characterized by many as unfounded and disrespectful of God's Word. Admittedly, Brunner overstated his case in the last sentence, not realizing how widely the view of inerrancy was held in the United States. But the main thrust of the criticism is that the doctrine of inerrancy has not faced up squarely to all the facts, and as a result it has become "the butt of scientific criticism." To be sure, scientific criticism is not inerrant, but, on the other hand, should we not earnestly reexamine our interpretation of the evidence to see whether or not Brunner's comment has some validity? We would do well to have the attitude of mind and spirit described in the following statement by Everett F. Harrison: "It would seem that the only healthy attitude for conservatives is to welcome criticism and be willing to join in it. No view of Scripture can indefinitely be sustained if it runs counter to the facts. That the Bible claims inspiration is patent. The problem is to define the nature of that inspiration in the light of the phenomena contained therein." [6]

Genesis, Ch. 5

Chapter 5 in Genesis contains the genealogy of man from Adam on through the three sons of Noah: Shem, Ham, and Japheth. The interpretation of the chapter varies from individual to individual; but regardless of this, the pattern of the writer is clear. He gives the age of a man at the birth of his son, how much longer he lived after that, and finally his age at death. On the strength of this and other genealogies in the Old Testament the Jewish and Christian communities reckoned the date of creation.

Since the numbers in the Hebrew and Septuagint texts vary, the two systems vary as well. The year 1963, being the year 5723 in Jewish tradition, puts the creation in 3760 B.C. On the other hand, many Christians have accepted the date 4004 B.C., determined by Archbishop James Ussher (1581–1656).

It was not until the nineteenth century that enough evidence was available to disprove the 4004 date as the beginning of the world, and even today many Bibles still carry the old chronology. During the latter part of the nineteenth century, however, some evangelical scholars became aware of the problem and attempted to reckon with it. The genealogies of Genesis, according to these studies, were to be considered trustworthy only for the purpose which the Biblical compiler had in mind. This issue hinged, therefore, on one's interpretation of the compiler's intent.

We do not know who worked up the material as it is in our Bible. Whether it was Moses or someone else, he certainly did so on the basis of ancient records or oral tradition. If he intended the genealogy merely as a survey highlighting the main men in the long history of the pre-Flood world, why did he retain, evidently from his sources, the three precise numbers of years (age at birth of son, years lived afterward, and age at death) for each of the men named? True, the ancient Orientals were selective in their genealogies at times, but when doing so, they did not pay such close attention to exact figures as in Gen., ch. 5. A selective list may have been the intent at the beginning of the oral tradition that transmitted the information, but it is hard to reconcile this intent with the specific figures which are an integral part of the present list. When the writer claims that Adam lived 130 years and then begat Seth, and that he lived 800 years afterward, making his total age 930 years, it is apparent that the writer intended the figures literally.

Until geological information disproved the 4004 date, most Jews and Christians (including many alert, even brilliant, persons) thought the genealogy in Gen., ch. 5, was intended to show the consecutive history of man. Inasmuch as some evangelicals in the nineteenth century felt the force of the new geological information, they were inclined to stretch the genealogy enough to provide gaps for the scientific data. But how did this relate to the intent of the author? If the geological and other scientific data known today had not been made available to us, would we have doubted that Gen., ch. 5, was intended to be chronological? Not likely. The Biblical evidence is too explicit at this point. It is our scientific knowledge that causes us to ignore the clear meaning of the passage. Obviously, then, the intent of the Biblical writer can hardly be accommodated to the scientific facts made available from generation to generation.

Acts 7:4

Stephen's speech before the council, which appears in Acts 7:2-53, begins with the details of Abraham's call. In v. 4, Stephen states: " Then he departed from the land of the Chaldeans, and lived in Haran. And after his father died, God removed him from there into this land in which you are now living." According to Gen. 11:26, Terah was 70 at the birth of Abraham, and he died in Haran at the age of 205 (ch. 11:32). Abraham, therefore, was 135 at the death of his father. However, Abraham left Canaan when he was 75 (ch. 12:4), sixty years before the death of his father. On what grounds, then, does Stephen declare that Abraham left for Canaan " after his father died "? Neither the Hebrew nor the Septuagint supports this claim.

This same idea is found in the writings of Philo, the Jewish scholar at Alexandria. Apparently Stephen and Philo were drawing from some kind of oral tradition that was alive in Judaism and the early church. Most likely Stephen's Jewish audience did not pick any flaws in his historical survey because they shared the same interpretation of history from the factual point of view.

It is difficult to determine why Philo, a student of the Pentateuch, believed that Abraham left Haran after his father died, because neither the Hebrew nor the Greek texts (as we have them now) would support such an interpretation. Possibly he had access to a Greek text that had Terah dying at 145 instead of

205. In any event there is strong evidence to show that it formed a part of an oral tradition.

Further support for this conclusion is found in Acts 7:23, where Stephen says Moses was forty years old when he felt he should visit his own people. This too is found in Philo, not in the Old Testament. Moreover, Stephen added in v. 25, " He supposed that his brethren understood that God was giving them deliverance by his hand, but they did not understand." This concept is not based on any Old Testament passage, and so it may well be another bit of the traditional interpretation of that day.

Stephen, after all, was speaking with his very life at stake. He had no scrolls to consult. He spoke out of the fullness of his heart and the store of information in his mind. He thought he was portraying a correct historical picture, and evidently his audience did too, but again honesty of intent does not rectify the difficulty. There is hardly any way out but to admit that Stephen, even while under the inspiration of the Holy Spirit, probably made a mistake in declaring that Abraham left Haran after Terah died.

Acts 7:15-16

Another statement in Stephen's speech demands attention also. In vs. 15-16 we read, " And he [Jacob] died, himself and our fathers, and they were carried back to Shechem and laid in the tomb that Abraham had bought for a sum of silver from the sons of Hamor in Shechem." Jacob was buried at Hebron (Mamre) in the field of Machpelah (Gen. 50:13), which Abraham had purchased from Ephron the Hittite (Gen. 23:16-18). Joseph, on the other hand, was buried at Shechem in the plot of ground which Jacob had purchased from the sons of Hamor (Josh. 24:32). According to Josephus (*Antiquities* II, 8, 2), all the sons of Jacob, except Joseph, were buried at Hebron.

This is the Old Testament and traditional evidence. What can we make of Stephen's statement? One of the most popular explanations of the older commentators was that of Daniel Whitby, which Matthew Henry quotes in his commentary: "*Jacob went down into Egypt and died, he and our fathers;* and (*our fathers*) *were carried over into Sychem; and he,* that is, *Jacob,* was laid *in the sepulchre that Abraham bought for a sum of money,* Gen. xxiii 16. (Or, they laid there, that is, Abraham, Isaac, and Jacob.) *And they,* namely, the other patriarchs, were *buried in the sepulchre bought of the sons of Emmor, the father of Sychem.*" [7] Thus, Whitby splits the verse up and supplies words to make Stephen mean what Genesis and Joshua say.

Others solve the difficulty by regarding the name "Abraham" as a scribal error for "Jacob," supposedly the original wording of the text. This conjecture, however, is without any textual basis. Still others, recognizing the weight of the textual evidence, suggest the possibility that Jacob bought again at a later time a field previously purchased by Abraham. The better part of wisdom is to accept the evidence we have, and frankly admit, as F. F. Bruce does, "The two purchases of land are telescoped here in much the same way as two separate calls of Abraham are telescoped in v. 2 and two separate Pentateuchal quotations in v. 7." [8]

Some commentators readily acknowledge that Stephen was mistaken, but they claim inerrancy for the autograph of The Acts in that Luke accurately copied Stephen's words, mistakes and all. However, this easy answer ignores the clear Biblical statement that Stephen spoke under the influence of the Holy Spirit. The difficulty, as Bruce implies, may well have arisen with Luke when he condensed Stephen's sermon. But with respect to the doctrine of inerrant autographs it makes no essential difference whether the telescoping occurred in Stephen's original speech or in Luke's condensation.

Galatians 3:17

In Gal. 3:16-17 of his letter to the churches of Galatia, Paul writes: "Now the promises were made to Abraham and to his offspring. It does not say, 'And to offsprings,' referring to many;

but, referring to one, 'And to your offspring,' which is Christ. This is what I mean: the law, which came four hundred and thirty years afterward, does not annul a covenant previously ratified by God, so as to make the promise void." All the Greek manuscripts have 430, so in all likelihood Paul's original letter had it as well. There is a problem with this figure, however. Abraham was 75 when he went to Canaan (Gen. 12:4), he was 100 when Isaac was born (ch. 21:5), Isaac was 60 when Jacob was born (ch. 25:26), and Jacob was 130 when he went to Egypt (ch. 47:9). Adding together 25, 60, and 130 gives 215 years in Canaan. The Hebrew text of Ex. 12:40 notes, "The time that the people of Israel dwelt in Egypt was four hundred and thirty years." Therefore, the time from the promise to Abraham to the giving of the law was 645 years (215 + 430). Did Paul get his information from another source, or did he mean something else when he wrote the number 430?

The Septuagint of Ex. 12:40 reads, "The time that the people of Israel dwelt in Egypt and in the land of Canaan was four hundred and thirty years." Thus, the Greek translation allots 215 years to Canaan and 215 to Egypt. It is quite possible, therefore, that Paul was following the LXX figure.

Another concern is the question whether the Hebrew or the LXX is correct. While the genealogies indicate only four generations from Levi through Moses, the preponderance of evidence which archaeology offers at the present time favors the 430-year stay in Egypt as noted in the Hebrew text.

Paul's reference to "the promises" is, according to one interpretation, a reference to the entire patriarchal period down to Jacob's descent into Egypt. Similarly "the law" is taken to mean the period beginning with Moses and the exodus. Granting this interpretation of the passage, Paul was correct and in accord with the Hebrew text of Ex. 12:40.

But Paul's argument in Gal. 3:16-17 hinges not on periods of time but on events in Israel's history. At first he relates the promises both to Abraham and to his descendants, but later he makes his intention clear by referring to "a covenant . . . ratified by

God." What else could this have meant to Paul's readers except the personal covenant that God made with Abraham, ratifying his previous promises? This dramatic event is described in Gen., ch. 15. After the details are noted, v. 18 summarizes, "On that day the LORD made a covenant with Abram." The sign of the covenant, circumcision, came later (Gen. 17:10). Inasmuch as these historic episodes took place within twenty-four years after Abraham arrived in Canaan, the span of time between it and the giving of the law on Mt. Sinai would logically include the 215 years of Canaan and the 430 in Egypt.

What justification is there, then, for interpreting Paul to mean 430 years after the patriarchal period closed (that is, when Jacob went to Egypt)? Had he wanted to say this, would he not have expressed himself more explicitly? As noted previously, Paul used the Septuagint a great deal, so why should one doubt its use here? In fact, because most of his readers probably read the Septuagint, the reference to 430 years would agree with their understanding of history and not distract their minds, therefore, from his main point. Evidently it seemed good to the Holy Spirit to let Paul use the traditional 430 years without informing him that he was technically wrong and should be using 645 years as found in the Hebrew.

Mark 14:30, 72

In Mark 14:30 Jesus says to Peter, "Truly, I say to you, this very night, before the cock crows twice, you will deny me three times." In v. 72 of the same chapter we read: "And immediately the cock crowed a second time. And Peter remembered how Jesus had said to him, 'Before the cock crows twice, you will deny me three times.'"

This same pattern (prediction by Jesus, occurrence of the event, and Peter's remembrance of the prediction) is also found in Matthew (ch. 26:34, 74-75) and Luke (ch. 22:34, 60-61). However, both of these accounts omit the words "twice," "second time," and "twice." In short, they report that Jesus said, "Before the cock crows, you will deny me three times."

In explaining the difference in detail in Mark's report of the denial episode, some evangelical scholars suggest that Matthew and Luke generalized the cock's crowing twice to mean "shall not have finished crowing." But why generalize if they knew the cock crowed twice?

Another explanation is the claim that the difficult reading is due to a scribal error. True, the Sinaiticus manuscript of the Greek New Testament omits the words "twice" and "second." In some other manuscripts the word "twice" or "second" is omitted in one or two cases, but never in all three occurrences. Moreover, the majority of the high quality manuscripts of Mark have "twice" or "second" in all three places.

Furthermore, there is no evidence to suggest that the words "twice" and "second" crept into the text on the basis of some later tradition. How is it that this supposed tradition spread through practically all the Greek manuscripts of Mark and yet had no influence in Matthew and Luke? What basis would there be for any scribe's attempt to insert the words into the text? There is plenty of reason, on the other hand, why a scribe would want to omit the words from Mark and thus harmonize it with the other two Gospels. Mark makes good sense as it is. The source of the scribal activity was most likely Mark himself as he took down bits of information from Peter's lips. The strong probability is that the words "twice" and "second" were in the autograph of Mark.

But what essential difference is there if the other Gospel writers, Matthew and Luke, follow the general tradition of the cock's crowing just once? All three Gospels contain the historical features necessary to convey the truth of the matter: the prediction of denial and Peter's boast, the fulfillment of the prediction, and Peter's remorse on remembering Jesus' words.

I Corinthians 3:19

Paul, in writing to the church at Corinth, said: "For the wisdom of this world is folly with God. For it is written, 'He catches the wise in their craftiness'" (ch. 3:19). The source of the quotation is Job 5:13, which is part of the first speech of Eliphaz the Temanite. Traditionally speaking, Eliphaz has never been considered as inspired. Job, so it is claimed, was the inspired one and he recorded the addresses of Eliphaz and his friends, errors and all.

Certain evangelicals more or less equate the expressions "It is written" and "God says." It cannot mean this in I Cor. 3:19 if Eliphaz is uninspired. Apparently Paul did not care who said it, nor whether he was inspired. The statement was true as far as he was concerned and so he used it in his argument. This illustration does not involve an error as such, but it does show how Biblical evidence is often at variance with some of the more precise formulations of inspiration. As Carnell observes, "Whether orthodoxy realized it or not, it was really saying that inspiration, at times, ensures no more than an infallible account of error." [9]

Inerrancy and Consistency

While the specific problems considered thus far in this chapter by no means exhaust the difficulties that Biblical phenomena present to Christians, they are sufficiently varied and precise to show the seriousness of the issue. The question is, What are we to make of these findings? The evidence can be viewed from three possible points of view: (1) Scripture teaches the doctrine of inerrancy, but the phenomena of Scripture disprove this claim; (2) Scripture teaches the doctrine of inerrancy, therefore any contradictions or errors are in appearance only; and (3) Scripture does not teach the doctrine of inerrancy, therefore the phenomena of Scripture are to be accepted as an important factor in determining a Biblical view of inspiration.

The first point of view frankly acknowledges that Scripture is not consistent in all the evidence relevant to the doctrine of inspiration. While some within the church accept this conclusion, the majority of Christians take either the second or third of the possible interpretations. The basic premise of these latter views is that God, being the author of all truth, was consistent in his revelation.

The determinative factor for the second point of view is the assurance that Scripture teaches the doctrine of inerrancy. The probability of some errors in the autographs is intolerable, therefore, because a perfect God would never have allowed such a thing to happen. As a result, the usual mood is one of caution with respect to the interpretation of the phenomena. Problems are recognized, but there is little inclination to resolve them on the basis of the evidence at hand. Let us not be hasty, so the argument goes, because we do not have all the information. Maybe future discoveries will resolve these apparent contradictions. But is such a fond hope justified? A number of scholars who hold to inerrancy recognize that some of the Biblical phenomena cannot be harmonized without employing strained or forced methods. This intellectual honesty is to be commended, but this series of suspended judgments indicates that the totality of Biblical evidence does not prove the doctrine of inerrancy to be a fact. It is still a theory that must be accepted by faith.

This conclusion is also supported by the kind of apologetic that is usually employed to parry the thrusts of the phenomena. The chief refutation is a negative one which concentrates on some glaring examples of error that the liberals have made. A favorite target is the German critic Anton F. Hartmann, who said that Moses could not have written the Pentateuch because the Hebrews did not start writing until the period of the Judges. Now we know that the Hebrews were literate and capable of writing from Abraham on down. Another example is early liberalism's verdict that Isa. 20:1 was erroneous in mentioning Sargon, a king otherwise unknown. Since that time a mass of information about Sargon, including his annals, has been discovered.

Of course, the idea back of such an argument is that in numerous instances liberalism has been proved wrong and in due time it will be proved wrong everywhere. But will this suggestion stand up under close scrutiny? The most extreme liberals today recognize the folly of these early statements. In many instances it has been the liberal camp itself that has corrected its earlier excesses. Many of the so-called "assured results" of higher criticism have proved to be "assumed results," but the evidence does not warrant the conclusion that this will happen to *all* of the liberal findings. In some instances, the so-called "assured results" of *tradition* are in reality "assumed results."

Truth is like a two-way street or a double-edged sword. Although facts confirm the Biblical record in many instances, they also disprove it in other cases. In the last analysis we must let the truth cut both ways. If we try to hold to the teaching of Scripture in preference to the phenomena, are we not saying in effect, "Determine the Biblical writers' doctrine of inspiration from what they say, not what they do"? The true Biblical view of inspiration must account for all the evidence of Scripture. The peril of the view of inerrancy is its rigidity and all-or-nothing character. If only one of the illustrations discussed in this chapter is correct, the doctrine is invalidated.

Inerrancy and Reason

Accordingly, the basic premise of the second point of view, the assurance that Scripture teaches the doctrine of inerrancy, needs to be reexamined. As noted earlier, those who hold this view believe in coming to the Bible as the source for determining doctrinal issues, but because the explicit teaching on inspiration is rather general in nature, they try to determine the implications of the Biblical writers. As Everett F. Harrison acknowledges: "Inerrancy is not a formally stated claim made by the Scriptures on their own behalf. It is rather an inference that devout students of the Word have made from the teaching of the Bible about its own inspiration."[10] It is at this very point, however, where there is an unconscious shift from the inductive to the deductive method. The assumption that God had to reveal himself inerrantly becomes determinative for interpretation. Thus it is claimed that Jesus believed and taught the doctrine of inerrancy. This view is to be accepted on the authority of Christ whether or not it accords with all the facts. But this is reasoning in a circle, of course, because the doctrine of inerrancy has attributed its own ideas to Jesus and then turned around to claim as its authority its own interpretation of what Jesus taught.

The only way to break out of this circular reasoning (with its implicit claim of inerrant interpretation) is to employ our reason objectively with respect to all the evidence, Biblical and otherwise. At the same time, however, we must acknowledge that perfect objectivity is never achieved. In spite of our sincere efforts we bring to the task of interpretation certain unconscious presuppositions that have become a part of us during our formative years. Yet, having made this concession, we are nonetheless dependent on reason; for we must use it to help isolate and set aside, as far as possible, even our restricting assumptions. The extent to which we can do this will determine the objectivity with which we can interpret the evidence at hand.

An appeal to the use of reason usually draws objections on the ground that reason is human and necessarily carnal. It is not uncommon to have the person who appeals to reason characterized as one who goes through his Bible underlining the true passages (presumably the portions he prefers) with one color, and the erroneous passages (those which he dislikes for one reason or another) with a different color. No doubt such arbitrary treatment of Scripture has occurred, but this is not a true picture of committed Christians who make a place for reason. One cannot rule out a legitimate use of human reason aided by the Holy Spirit on the grounds that unaided reason leads to serious error and eventually considers the gospel as foolishness.

Another objection to reason and its right to detect error is that man becomes thereby the arbiter of truth and error. But this argument fails to see that the human mind does not create the evidence which is determinative in the separation of truth from error. All human reason can do is to function properly with the data that are furnished it. Every human being has the power and the right to observe the data. The factor of truth or error is settled before human reason comes on the scene. While reason can function correctly with the evidence and ascertain the true and the false, it is also possible for it to work improperly and to come to inaccurate evaluation of the data. In neither case, however, is human reason the *real* arbiter of truth or error.

Ultimately there can be no valid objection to the use of reason. Every reader of Scripture uses his reason to some extent. The "inference" leading to the doctrine of inerrancy involves reason, but it is the deductive method. Reason is indispensable; the crucial factor is *how* we use it, not that we do. In highlighting the basic issue between true doctrine (the correct use of reason) and one's definition of doctrine (the faulty use of reason), Evans declares: "If the theories of other days will not bear the pressure of . . . facts, they must go to the wall. There is no help for it. If your definition of inspiration, your definition of the infallibility of the Bible — mark what I say! not the doctrine, but your definition of the doctrine — if that definition will not stand the test of the established results of criticism, if it will not harmonize with ascertained facts, then so much the worse for the definition."[11]

Those evangelical Christians who do not find the doctrine of inerrancy in Scripture are free to recognize that the phenomena indicate the presence of some errors in the autographs (for example, the erroneous synchronisms of II Kings, chs. 17 and 18). Instead of trying to determine implications of the text and to fill in areas of silence, they emphasize the explicit teachings of Scripture. In this way there is no need to choose between teaching and phenomena. They both arrive at the same conclusion.

False in One, False in All

During the last twenty years or so there has been an increasing awareness of the difficulties facing the doctrine of inerrancy and some have felt an inclination to follow the phenomena and explicit teaching of Scripture. At the same time there has usually been a reluctance to make the change on account of the haunting fear implicit in the legal maxim, "False in one, false in all." If a person on the witness stand proves to be inaccurate in his testimony in one instance, the presumption is that he may be inaccurate in other places as well. The presumption is even greater in case of perjury because the intent to deceive involves a whole series of falsehoods. In no case, however, is this legal rule-of-thumb adhered to rigidly in the courts. On what authority, then, must this principle be applied with absolute consistency to the Scriptures?

The tradition of this maxim in theological circles goes back at least to the sixteenth century. Laelius Socinus (1525–1562), a very brilliant and inquisitive person, left his homeland Italy in 1544 and went to Switzerland. There he put many difficult questions to Calvin, who rebuked him for his "luxurious inquisitiveness" and urged him to correct his ways. In 1575 his nephew, Faustus Socinus (1539–1604), left Italy to come to Basel, Switzerland. He not only inherited his uncle's unpublished manuscripts, but he also accepted some of his uncle's views, the most heretical being his rejection of Christ as part of the Trinity: in short, God, he held, was a unity.

This unitarian heresy set Socinus at odds with both the Reformed and the Lutheran theologians. Oddly enough, however, Socinus was pretty much of a literalist and he contended that if a person could doubt concerning one passage, there was no reason why he could not doubt concerning all of them. In the bitter battle that ensued between Socinus and the Lutherans, his opponents accepted his dictum and thus was begun the challenge to prove just one error.

Once the method of reasoning became grounded in the maxim, "False in one, false in all," it was inevitable that the issue of inspiration would become an either-or: either the autographs were inerrant, or else human fallibility infected all of Scripture. Consistency would permit no mediating point of view. Either the inerrancists were right or the rank liberals.

The dedication of J. Gresham Machen's highly respected book *What Is Faith?* reads: "TO FRANCIS LANDEY PATTON this book is dedicated as an inadequate but heartfelt expression of gratitude and respect." Patton (1843–1932) was president of Princeton University from 1888 to 1902, and president of Princeton Theological Seminary from 1902 to 1913. Concerning this either-or position, Patton declares: "The trouble is that there is a disposition on the part of some, apparently, to show that unless the Bible is inerrantly accurate in everything, you cannot trust it for anything. There are those who seem to say that the order of a man's thought must be first the inspired Bible and secondly the divine Christ. To that position I cannot consent; and I am unable to make the *in terrorem* argument that unless you believe in the inerrancy of the Bible, you have no right to believe in Christ. It is surely a strange apologetic that says, 'Faith in Christ is all you need for salvation'; and then says, 'You have no right to your faith in Christ unless you believe that the Bible is without error.' Moreover, a more fallacious argument could not be used than that which is sometimes employed in a misuse of the legal maxim, *Falsus in uno, falsus in omnibus.* How much history could stand this test? The real question is whether the Bible is true, not whether it is inspired. Must a book on every subject be inspired in order to be true? Have we lost all faith in inductive logic? Have we abandoned human testimony as a source of information? Is there no longer a place for the common sense of mankind?"[12] While some evangelicals regret this so-called low view of inspiration, they confess, nevertheless, that there is much good in Patton's book. But how can one accept the "much good" when, according to the maxim, "False in one, false in all," the unfortunate (presumably inaccurate) statements lead to the logical conclusion that nothing in Patton's book can be trusted? Evidently the maxim applies only to Scripture.

Rationality and Irrationality

Inasmuch as method implies a process of reasoning it is valid to inquire how far human reason and logic can go in solving the problem of inspiration. We have seen that logic has been a basic tool in developing the theory of inerrancy. But logic founded on a false premise can lead to exceedingly erroneous conclusions; for example, the assumption " error = no inspiration." The Bible, however, does not teach that unless a thing is *totally* true it cannot be inspired. Therefore, when this rational dogma is confronted with the Biblical data it finds the going quite difficult. It is usually at this point that those who hold to inerrancy become irrationalists. They speak of the disturbing facts as an area of " mystery " and suggest withholding judgment. Sooner or later we all come to a point of mystery and we do well to acknowledge that we have entered the suprarational realm, but the crucial question is where this transition is made. Whereas the logical system of inerrancy must dismiss logic when it comes to Biblical phenomena, those who hold to a strong doctrine of inspiration, without accepting inerrancy, can accept all the facts, even though they are not always able to explain the precise relationship of the data. In other words, if reason is to play any part in determining the doctrine of inspiration, we must allow it to go as far as it can. Patton comments on this point: " You cannot license Reason to seek truth and deny her right to see error. And it is a hazardous thing to say that being inspired the Bible must be free from error; for then the discovery of a single error would destroy its inspiration. Nor have we any right to substitute the word ' inerrancy ' for ' inspiration ' in our discussion of the Bible unless we are prepared to show from the teaching of the Bible that inspiration means inerrancy — and that, I think, would be a difficult thing to do." [13]

According to Patton, therefore, the primary task of inspiration was not to secure the inerrancy of the record. His views are considered with alarm, however, for he is supposedly splitting the rock foundation on which Christianity rests. But the crack that appears is not in the foundation; it is only in the encrustations of interpretation which have been added gradually.

"The Bible as Divining Rod"

As a postscript to this discussion of the phenomena of Scripture a word of caution is in order concerning some relatively recent statements by the world-famous archaeologist Dr. Nelson Glueck. In an article, "The Bible as Divining Rod," he relates how archaeology has thrown much light on Biblical passages and, in turn, how the Bible has aided archaeologists in making new discoveries. "It is worth emphasizing," writes Glueck, "that in all this work no archaeological discovery has ever controverted a single, properly understood Biblical statement."[14] Many who hold to the doctrine of inerrancy have taken comfort in this assertion, for it appears that one of the foremost Biblical scholars has spoken out in their behalf. In order to ascertain the precise meaning and implications of this claim, the author of this book questioned Dr. Glueck personally. The latter made it quite plain that he had no intention of supporting the doctrine of inerrancy. His primary concern is to point out "the amazing accuracy of historical memory in the Bible."[15]

Deuteronomy 8:9, for example, refers to Canaan as "a land whose stones are iron, and out of whose hills you can dig copper." This would not be true if the "land" meant only traditional Canaan "from Dan to Beersheba" (Judg. 20:1), but the Bible also speaks of Israel's boundaries as extending "from the entrance of Hamath to the Brook of Egypt" (I Kings 8:65). Understood in this larger perspective, the claim in Deut. 8:9 is indeed accurate, for the copper mines of Solomon have been found in the Wadi of the Arabah, south of the Dead Sea.

The vindication of this and many other Biblical passages has led Glueck to affirm that the Bible "can be regarded in effect as an almost infallible divining rod, revealing to the expert the whereabouts and characteristics of lost cities and civilizations."[16] Again, however, this statement cannot be taken as supporting the doctrine of inerrancy. It is conditioned by "almost," and also it relates primarily to the geography of Palestine and the Near East. The Pekah problem, on the other hand, involves an interpretation of data which the historian did not completely understand and which he had no means of verifying. While Glueck is convinced of the amazing accuracy and essential trustworthiness of Scripture, he readily acknowledges that the Biblical writers were not inerrant historians. He is a friend of all those who cherish Scripture, but he cannot be claimed as a champion of the doctrine of inerrancy.

5: *Verbal Inspiration*

CLOSELY RELATED to the concept of inerrancy is the idea of verbal inspiration. Various interpretations have been given to the term " verbal," but generally speaking, this view conceives of inspiration as extending to the individual words of Scripture.

Jeremiah, Ch. 36

As noted previously, the clearest description of the origin of a canonical book is to be found in Jer., ch. 36. Jeremiah is told by the LORD to take a scroll and write on it " all the words that I have spoken to you against Israel and Judah and all the nations, from the day I spoke to you, from the days of Josiah until today " (v. 2). This message came to Jeremiah in 605 B.C. (the fourth year of Jehoiakim) and he was ordered to put in writing all God had said to him from the day of his call in 626 B.C. (the thirteenth year of Josiah).

The account informs us that Jeremiah called Baruch, his scribe, who then wrote on the scroll " at the dictation of Jeremiah [literally, " from the mouth of Jeremiah "] all the words of the LORD which he had spoken to him " (v. 4). Some have interpreted this verse to mean that God " dictated " the words to Jeremiah. However, this assumption has no basis in the Biblical account. The Hebrew text does not say that Jeremiah was dictating the words that the LORD *was speaking* to him. Rather, Jeremiah dictates the words that the LORD *had spoken* to him previously. Jeremiah must have repeated some of the oracles of God time and time again, so that after twenty-one years the basic themes were well fixed in his mind. The memory of the ancient Oriental was exceedingly well developed, therefore there is no need to postulate "dictation by God" during the recording of the oracles given previously.

Another factor to be considered is the use of the word "all" in vs. 2 and 4. Evidently it was intended extensively. Jeremiah could very well have dictated from memory messages covering in extent the whole of God's oracles to him. Undoubtedly some of the words that the LORD spoke to Jeremiah during the twenty-one-year period were omitted from Jeremiah's first book, for in ch. 36:32 we read, "Baruch . . . wrote . . . at the dictation of Jeremiah all the words of the scroll which Jehoiakim king of Judah had burned in the fire; and many similar words were added to them." These "similar words" must have been some aspects of God's oracles which did not occur to Jeremiah at the writing of the first book.

Inspiration of the Person

In any case, whether one interprets the text to mean God dictated to Jeremiah or not, there can be no doubt that Jeremiah was the inspired one. It is implicit, of course, that Baruch made a trustworthy record of what Jeremiah dictated; however, nothing is made of this point. If the writer of ch. 36 (presumably Baruch) had been thinking primarily of the book as being inspired, he would probably have said "God wrote on the scroll," just as Jeremiah's sayings elsewhere are often introduced with the expression, "God says." On the contrary, the emphasis is on Jeremiah, the channel of God's words. The written words are inspired because their source was inspired.

After the burning of the first scroll by Jehoiakim, Jeremiah was told to take a second scroll and "write on it all the former words that were in the first scroll" (ch. 36:28). God gave Jeremiah an additional oracle against Jehoiakim (ch. 36:29-31) because of his insolent deed, but there is nothing in the text which authorizes Jeremiah to add "many similar words." It is implicit that these were primarily portions of previous oracles that had not occurred to Jeremiah at the composition of the first book.

Inspiration of the Book

Those who have held to the doctrine of verbal inspiration have never doubted the inspiration of the person as the channel of revelation, but because of other Biblical evidence and certain difficulties inherent in an emphasis on the person, they have generally preferred to speak of the "inspired book." Preus summarizes the opinion of the seventeenth-century Lutheran theologians as follows: "Properly speaking, inspiration pertains to the holy Scriptures themselves. It may be said, however, that the writers too were inspired by God: they wrote by the illumination and inspiration of the Holy Ghost."[1]

One reason for stressing the inspiration of the book was the sporadic nature of the inspiration of a number of Biblical writers. David, for example, was inspired of God while producing his psalms. But when, after his sin in taking Bathsheba, he sent a letter to Joab the general, saying, "Set Uriah in the forefront of the hardest fighting, and then draw back from him, that he may be struck down, and die" (II Sam. 11:15), neither David nor his letter was inspired of God. Tradition has considered the writer of the book of Samuel as the inspired one. He gave an accurate copy of the letter that God intended to be included in Scripture.

While there is some justification for this distinction between the inspiration of the source of the Biblical material and the inspiration of the compiler of that material, the idea has been carried too far in some instances. According to some, Stephen was just a preacher who made mistakes in his survey of Israel's history, whereas Luke, preserving these errors, was the inspired one. Yet Luke does not claim inspiration for himself. His authorization for writing is not a command from God. He simply says, "It seemed good to me." Moreover, Luke does not consider his Gospel and history of the early church as inspired books. "An orderly account" is the only claim he makes.

The clearest evidence for defining inspiration in terms of the book comes from II Tim. 3:16. Paul says Scripture is *theopneustos,* "inspired by God." Because Paul was thinking in terms of the extant manuscripts, his primary emphasis was on the book, but this does not mean that Paul would deny the inspiration of the Old Testament writers. He would certainly agree with II Peter 1:21: "Men moved by the Holy Spirit spoke from God."

Even though the Biblical writers were not always inspired (David in his adultery, Solomon in his idolatry, Paul in his anger with Barnabas, and Peter in his duplicity at Antioch), it is evident that they were when God spoke through them. The totality of Biblical evidence seems to indicate that inspiration is involved in the whole process of God's revelation: the person, whether speaker or writer, and the message, whether oral or written. The book, the end result, is inspired because it is God's message, but there would have been no book if first there had not been an inspired channel. As Orr observes, "Inspiration belongs primarily to the *person,* and to the *book* only as it is the product of the inspired person." [2]

Verbal Inspiration and Matt. 5:17-18

Since the traditional doctrine of verbal inspiration has placed primary emphasis on the inspiration of the book, the tendency has been to interpret "verbal" as applying to each word of the Hebrew and Greek autographs. Perhaps the key passage adduced in support of this stress on individual words has been Jesus' declaration in Matt. 5:17-18. In preparation for his discussion on the law, Jesus assures his audience: "Think not that I have come to abolish the law and the prophets; I have come not to abolish them but to fulfil them. For truly, I say to you, till heaven and earth pass away, not an iota, not a dot, will pass from the law until all is accomplished." For the last part of v. 18, the King

James Version translates, " One jot or one tittle shall in no wise pass from the law, till all be fulfilled." Jesus intends to refute some Jewish interpretations of the law (" It has been said to you . . . , but I say to you "); therefore, he is very careful to preface his remarks with a statement expressing his confidence in the law. " Do not think for a moment," Jesus assures them, " that I have come to tear down the law or the prophets piece by piece. [The same verb is used in Matt. 24:2 concerning the Temple.] I have not come to tear down, but to fill to the full."

This law, Jesus affirmed, was as sure as " heaven and earth." To the Jewish mind this was the ultimate in stability, for as Ps. 89:29 stated, " I will establish his line for ever and his throne as the days of the heavens," and as Ps. 119:90 declared, " Thy faithfulness endures to all generations; thou hast established the earth, and it stands fast."

Jesus' use of the term " iota " (translated " jot " in the King James Version) is a reference to the Greek letter *iota,* which in turn goes back to the Hebrew letter *yod,* the smallest letter of the alphabet (in the Aramaic or square script that was commonly employed to write Hebrew from the third century B.C. on). The " tittle " or " dot " is a reference to the small features that distinguish certain letters of the Hebrew alphabet from other letters that are very similar in appearance. Jesus is making it clear, accordingly, that the smallest item of the law is important.

Not one of these items will pass from the law " until all is accomplished." From the King James translation " fulfilled " in v. 18, the reader would think the verb was the same as in the previous verse, but such is not the case. The Greek reads literally, " until all has become." The idea back of this " coming to be " is the *purpose* for which the law was given. So long as the heavens and the earth exist, so long will the law continue to work out or accomplish its purpose. Some portions of the law would " come to be " (that is, achieve their purpose — for example, the ceremonial law) and so pass away. Jesus was *not* saying that all the law would continue until the heavens and earth would be dissolved.

How, then, are we to interpret Jesus' use of " iota " and " dot "?

Traditionally, the passage has been taken to refer to the *words* of the law (a description for the whole Old Testament), and thus a witness for the doctrine of inerrant, verbal inspiration. But this view fails to take into account the fact that the Hebrew manuscripts of the Old Testament in Jesus' day swarmed with variant spellings and forms because of the omission or addition of *yods*. It is recognized that Jesus argued at times from the accuracy of specific words, but in this overall statement concerning the law, his emphasis can hardly be on the words or letters. The prevailing tendency of Jewish interpretation, to stress the letter instead of the spirit of the law, is the very thing Jesus is refuting in Matt. 5:17-48.

An illustration of Jewish concern for the very letters of the Hebrew text is a rabbinical comment on Ruth 3:14. The text reads, " So she lay at his feet until the morning, but arose before one could recognize another; and he said, 'Let it not be known that the woman came to the threshing floor.' " The Hebrew word translated " before " has the letter *waw,* a distinctive spelling not found elsewhere in the Old Testament. The Jewish commentators felt that the occurrence of the letter *waw* (which, as the sixth letter of the Hebrew alphabet, has the numerical value 6) was intended by God to inform the readers that Ruth lay on the threshing floor at Boaz' feet for *six hours*. But this explanation given to a scribal mistake is hardly proof of the author's intent in ch. 3:14.

Zeal for the letter, the object of Jesus' criticism, was also a plague to the apostle Paul. Legalists from Jerusalem and thereabouts visited the young churches that Paul had started and they caused great unrest among the young Christians. In his letter to the Romans he speaks of this vital issue: " He is a Jew who is one inwardly, and real circumcision is a matter of the heart, spiritual and not literal [the Greek reads " in spirit not in letter "] " (Rom. 2:29). In Rom. 7:6, Paul comments further, " We serve not under the old written code [Greek, " in oldness of letter "], but in the new life of the Spirit [Greek, " in newness of spirit "]." This concept is also treated in II Cor. 3:6, where Paul declares, God " qualified us to be ministers of a new covenant, not in a written code, but in the Spirit; for the written code kills, but the Spirit gives life." Thus Paul asserts with Jesus that the essence of the law is its spirit, the principles it embodies, not its letter. Accordingly, to interpret Jesus in Matt. 5:17-18 as pleading for the inerrancy of the smallest detail of the Old Testament is to misinterpret him.

Verbal Inspiration and I Cor. 2:1-16

Another key passage for the doctrine of inspiration is I Cor. 2:1-16. Since Paul's authority as a true apostle was being questioned by some in the church at Corinth, he took the pains to remind them that when he began working with them his speech and message "were not in plausible words of wisdom, but in demonstration of the Spirit and power" (ch. 2:4). The "secret and hidden wisdom of God" (ch. 2:7) was revealed, so Paul claims, "through the Spirit" (ch. 2:10). He explains further: "Now we have received not the spirit of the world, but the Spirit which is from God, that we might understand the gifts bestowed on us by God. And we impart this in words not taught by human wisdom but taught by the Spirit" (ch. 2:12-13). While Paul's claim here refers primarily to his *preaching,* he states later on in this same letter, "if any one thinks that he is a prophet, or spiritual, he should acknowledge that what I am writing to you is a command of the Lord" (ch. 14:37). Thus Paul attached as much authority to the written form of his message as to the oral.

While Paul appears to claim that his teaching was verbally inspired, not everything in his letters deals with the "secret and hidden wisdom" which God revealed to him. Can Paul's statement be extended to mean inerrancy of every detail of his writings? In ch. 1:14 of this same letter, Paul writes, "I am thankful that I baptized none of you except Crispus and Gaius." But two verses later Paul remembers others he baptized and so he inserts into his letter: "I did baptize also the household of Stephanas. Beyond that, I do not know whether I baptized any one else." If

v. 16 is correct, then v. 14 is not. If the "none of you except" in v. 14 was breathed to Paul by God, word for word, why did it have to be corrected? Paul's uncertainty as to just how many people he baptized in Corinth is hardly to be placed in the same category as his confidence regarding his teaching. It would appear, therefore, that in the New Testament, as in the Old, neither the phenomena nor the claims of the Biblical writers justify a strict doctrine of verbal inspiration.

Words or Ideas Inspired?

One of the vexing problems in the area of inspiration is the relationship between words and ideas. This issue exercised the Lutheran theologians of the seventeenth century a great deal. Their definitions varied slightly, but in general they made a clear distinction between words as form or symbols (called *materia*) and content or ideas (called *forma*) expressed by these symbols.

Yet having made this distinction, they still realized that the content could not be separated from the words. Preus, expressing the common view of the seventeenth-century Lutherans, writes, "The letters and words of Scripture not only signify the inspired content of the Scriptures but actually impart this divine meaning and therefore cannot be separated from it."[3] From a superficial reading of such statements one gets the feeling that the dogmaticians worshiped the very letter. But as Preus observes: "The efficacy of the Word of God does not inhere in the letters and syllables and words as they are written. These are merely symbols, the vehicle (*vehiculum*) of the divine content, the *forma,* of the Word which alone is the Word of God, properly speaking. The dogmaticians will have no part of that ancient superstition which supposed that the words of the Bible as words could cure sickness and exorcise devils. In medieval times it was the practice of some to carry the Bible on their shoulders in the hope that it would ward off evil spirits and calamities. Only the inspired content of the Word which is the mind and counsel of

God has the power to work conversion and other spiritual realities in man." [4]

During the last hundred years, however, it has become increasingly clear that one cannot separate words and ideas. The late John Baillie (1886–1960) quoted F. D. Maurice as expressing his own point of view: "When you speak to me of verbal *inspiration,* though I do not like the phrase, though it seems to me to involve a violent — a scarcely grammatical — ellipsis, yet I subscribe most unequivocally to the meaning which I suppose is latent in it. I have no notion of inspired thoughts which do not find for themselves a suitable clothing of words. I can scarcely, even in my mind, separate the language of a writer from his meaning. And I certainly find this difficulty greater in studying a book of the Bible than in studying any other book." [5]

B. F. Westcott expresses a similar view in the following, often-quoted passage: "The slightest consideration will show that words are as essential to intellectual processes as they are to mutual intercourse. For man, the purely spiritual and absolute is but an aspiration or a dream. Thoughts are wedded to words as necessarily as soul to body." [6] The truth of this statement is beyond question, but some very false implications have been drawn from it. Since ideas are wedded to words, it follows, according to some evangelicals, that inerrancy of ideas necessitates inerrancy of *all* words.

This conclusion, however, is only partially true. In Gal., ch. 3, for example, Paul argues for the supremacy of grace over law because the promise was given before the law. If he had inverted the words, arguing instead for the priority of the law, obviously the wrong words would have led to the wrong concept. But granting the necessity of correct *key* words does not imply inerrancy for all the words. Paul's argument holds true whether he says the law came 430 or 645 years after the promise to Abraham. Although Paul's reference to 430 years could technically be termed an incorrect "idea," it is a nonessential idea in relation to the primary issue that Paul is attempting to communicate. Accordingly, we must always keep in mind the distinction between the essentials and the nonessentials in Scripture.

Mark's account of Peter's denial is another good illustration of this principle. Whether the cock crowed once, twice, or a dozen times makes no essential difference as far as God's purpose and our response are concerned. This minor detail varied with the human memories of the writers, but all the writers agree on the basic facts.

As a universal truth, applicable to Biblical and non-Biblical literature alike, we may lay down the following principle: a true concept necessitates correct key words, but there may well be some inaccurate details that are incidental to the argument or presentation of the chief idea. Recognition of this fact is even found in the writings of most scholars who defend the doctrine of inerrancy or verbal inspiration, especially when they deal with such Biblical phenomena as variations in parallel accounts and differences between New Testament quotations and the Old Testament sources.

Calvin recognized the difficulty of squaring some of the New Testament quotations with their Old Testament sources. He frankly admitted that some quotations from the Septuagint involved inaccuracies, but his out was the claim that the incorrect portion of the quotation was never used to prove the writer's point. As Kenneth Kantzer comments: "Interestingly enough, Calvin argues that quotation of the Old Testament by the New Testament is no guarantee of the correct text of the Old Testament. The New Testament writer, however, never uses the incorrect element in the quotation to prove his point. Luke, for example, in quoting an inaccurate text from the Septuagint, is merely using the commonly accepted version with which folks were familiar. The point which Luke wishes to make, nevertheless, is derived from that part of the Septuagint text which is absolutely correct."[7] But does this line of reasoning prove the inerrancy of the erroneous words which were not involved in the argument?

Verbal Inspiration and Ideas

Because the term " verbal " has the unfortunate feature of seeming to claim inspiration for each separate word of the text, some conservative scholars have proposed what amounts to a doctrine emphasizing inerrancy of ideas. In parallel accounts, " verbal " agreement is not to be expected because the writers of Scripture never thought in terms of the precise accuracy associated with the scientific age. Calvin, for example, recognized this fact. After giving his explanation for differences between Matt. 21:10-22 and the parallel accounts in Mark and Luke, he says, " But anyone who will consider how little care the Evangelists bestowed on pointing out dates will not stumble at this diversity in the narrative."[8] Moreover, " verbal " exactness is not to be expected in quotations, because the interest of the New Testament writers centered in the *sense, not the exact wording,* of the Old Testament source. In effect, then, the term " verbal " is broadened so as to refer ultimately to ideas rather than to every word.

Verbal Inspiration and Truth

In conjunction with this broadened definition of " verbal," some have defined truth as that which corresponds to the nature and purpose of God. The expressed purpose of this new orientation has been to consider the problem of inerrancy in terms of standards current in Biblical times rather than to impose on Scripture the demands of twentieth-century accuracy. While this attempt may alleviate some of the difficulty inherent in the doctrine of inerrancy or verbal inspiration, it is not able to account for all the phenomena. Are the erroneous synchronisms in II Kings, chs. 17 and 18, for example, in accord with the nature and purpose of God? If so, why even raise the issue of inerrancy? If not, how can they be true?

Others have defined truth in terms of the intent of the Biblical writers. There is much to be said for this approach to the problem. When the Gospel writers compile events in topical fashion, one is not justified in expecting a precise historical sequence. No fault can be found with Luke when he changes the Jewish expression "kingdom of heaven" to "kingdom of God." On the other hand, what is one to make of Jude's quotation from the book of Enoch? If, as the text indicates, Jude believed his quotation was actually from the pre-Flood patriarch, how can his intent convert the misunderstanding into truth? The intent of the compiler of II Kings, chs. 17 and 18, was to inform the reader of the specific relationship that Hoshea and Hezekiah bore to each other, but his intent did not make it so.

Ultimately, therefore, truth must be defined in terms of reality or facts. Aside from this absolute formulation of truth, the doctrine of inerrancy is pointless. Regardless of the motivation or intent of the Biblical writers, if any portion of the Bible deviates from reality, it is far better to speak in terms of the essential accuracy and trustworthiness of Scripture. For a person in the period of transition there may be some psychological value in clinging to the term "inerrancy" while filling it with new meaning, but eventually this contradiction will have to be given up.

The older apologists for the doctrine of inerrancy realized that the view did not permit any exceptions. Therefore in practice their defense of the claim that every word of the autographs was breathed by God and protected from error usually took the form of a challenge to prove just one error. This is all the more reason why evangelical Christianity must shift its defense to the point where it has the protection of the facts. In terms of absolute truth, Jude was in error because his qualification "seventh from Adam" cannot withstand the test of reality. But this need not cause any alarm because the essential truth of Jude's argument does not hinge on the validity of his proof text. This same principle applies to some of the arguments employed by other Biblical writers as well. An excellent example is Matt. 2:14-15, which reads: "And he [Joseph] rose and took the child and his mother by night, and departed to Egypt, and remained there until the death of Herod. This was to fulfil what the Lord had spoken by the prophet, 'Out of Egypt have I called my son.'" The quotation is from Hos. 11:1, where the prophet, speaking for God, states, " When Israel was a child, I loved him, and out of Egypt I called my son." The context is a passage in which God is reiterating his gracious dealings with Israel in the past, one of the greatest being the deliverance from Egypt. The sense of the passage and the intention of the prophet point backward, not forward. There is not the slightest hint that the statement was intended as a prophecy.

Tradition has contended that any adaptation of the original is allowable as long as it proceeds by a true interpretation of the passage. The question is whether Matthew's use of Hos. 11:1 is really a true interpretation. It is also claimed that any neglect of the context of the original is allowable so long as the sense is not falsified. There was apparently a definite cause-and-effect relationship in the mind of Matthew and so he quoted the passage as being authoritative proof from the Old Testament for an event in the life of Jesus. Although unintentional, is not his use of Hos. 11:1 in a sense a distortion of the context? Is Matthew's appeal to Hosea actually true to the sense of the passage when he picks words out from the context and uses them for another purpose in the New Testament?

Christians today believe that Jesus Christ was the Son of God and that he was anticipated in the Old Testament, but they do so largely on the basis of observations and reports in the Biblical record. The essential truth of Matthew's account is not dependent on his proof-text method. This Jewish mode of thinking, so common to the first century A.D., was suited to Matthew's Jewish readers, but it has no validity for the twentieth-century mind that thinks in terms of precise accuracy. In other words, what Matthew was trying to demonstrate (namely, that Jesus of Nazareth was the promised Messiah, the Son of God) is true, but his method of proving his conviction does not conform to all the facts. Matthew's logic in this instance bears the mark of his day, and as such one is not compelled to accept his method of reasoning any more than one is required to wear sandals and a tunic in order to be a Christian. Inasmuch as erroneous nonessentials do not invalidate the essential truth, it is unnecessary to contend for the unique inspiration and accuracy of every word of the autographs. By shifting the line of defense from "absolute truth" to "essential truth," it is possible to reckon with all the phenomena and teaching of Scripture and to have a sound view of authority as well.

Verbal Inspiration and Dictation

While formulations of verbal inspiration have often been characterized by critics as the dictation view, the charge has been rejected repeatedly. The problem is well illustrated by the theologians of the seventeenth century. They declared, on the one hand, that every word in Scripture was inspired and dictated by God. On the other hand, they could claim with equal sincerity and feeling that the writers wrote willingly and without loss of their own styles and idioms. In short, God *accommodated* himself and his message to the intellect, emotions, natural endowments, and normal speech of ordinary men. Concerning this paradox, Preus comments: "If these two parallel thoughts seem paradoxical, if they seem to contradict each other, the orthodox teachers make no effort to harmonize them. Such a lacuna [blank, gap] in their theology will of course trouble those who study them, but the minute the dogmaticians are represented as crossing this lacuna they are certain to be misrepresented. This habit of blandly refraining from drawing what seem to be the logical consequences of their tenets was not uncommon among the Lutheran theologians of the sixteenth and seventeenth centuries; in fact, it was a principle with them."[9]

While those who have made formulations of the doctrine of verbal inspiration during the nineteenth and twentieth centuries have been quite aware of the inherent paradox, still the claim has been made that every word of Scripture is equally from man as it is from God. How each word can stem from a free, responsible individual and still be God's intended communication is frankly admitted to be a mystery. Indeed, Scripture does not tell us the mode or means by which God revealed his message to his inspired servants, but is not this fact good reason for refraining from any claim of inerrancy in Scripture? Jude's qualification "seventh from Adam" is *man's word* because it represents the opinion current in his day. But how can it be *God's word* at the same time when it is not in accord with the facts? Although the Holy Spirit did not overrule the erroneous words, this does not mean that God was responsible for placing the words in the mind of Jude.

Notwithstanding repeated denials of the charge, the doctrine of inerrancy leads eventually into the mechanical or dictation theory of inspiration. God could not have given a verbally inerrant Scripture through human channels without dictating the correct information directly to the Biblical writers where they or their sources were in error.

Verbal Inspiration and Language

Another issue pertaining to the doctrine of verbal inspiration (defined broadly to include both the words and the ideas wedded to them) has to do with the characteristics of language. Can one legitimately speak of human language as being capable of inerrant communication from God? Undoubtedly God was capable of thinking in terms of Hebrew, so direct communication with the prophets did not involve the difficulties inherent in translations. However, unless God dictated his revelation word for word, there is no assurance that the Old Testament writers caught all the nuances or overtones of God's self-disclosure. Words are symbols that cover areas of meaning, and the area varies from individual to individual, depending on the background or experience of the person (for example, the complex terms "capitalist" and "communist"). Consequently no two people speaking the same language necessarily mean the same thing by the same word. In the process of any extended communication something is added to, or deleted from, the precise meaning intended by the communicator.

Scripture is no exception to this linguistic fact. Certainly this is true of the metaphorical language that had to be employed in expressing those spiritual realities extending beyond the realms of the five senses. Furthermore, in the case of biography, or even autobiography, language cannot possibly convey to the reader all the facets of personality and character of the individual under discussion. How much less could words describe the incarnate Christ completely. For this reason we should always bear in mind the difference between Jesus, the living Word, and Scripture, the written Word.

Yet from the symbolism of metaphorical language the human mind is able to distill concepts which amount to literal truth. Although some would describe these concepts as "absolute truth," they are more properly classified as truths about absolutes. In any case, *effective* communication has always been possible. In spite of the marred "image of God" in mankind, regenerate man has always had the mental and spiritual qualities requisite for receiving communications from Scripture and also for communicating these spiritual truths to his fellowmen. With the aid of the Holy Spirit the Scriptures have always been able to communicate sufficient truth to meet the needs of the sincere, inquiring reader. On the other hand, since language is incapable of absolute communication, we are hardly warranted in describing Scripture in terms of inerrancy. As Westcott put it, "For man, the purely spiritual and absolute is but an aspiration or a dream."

6: *Plenary Inspiration and the Canon*

DURING the last century or so, the doctrine of inerrancy has been known generally as the " verbal plenary " view of inspiration. It is necessary now to turn our attention to the " plenary " aspect of this formulation. The term comes from the Latin *plenus,* " full." According to the plenary view, every word of the autographs was equally inspired.

This general statement does not become definitive, however, unless precise limits are set. To speak of *fullness* of inspiration one must determine which books come under the category. " Canon," the usual term for designating the limits of the Bible, comes from a Greek word meaning " straight rod," " bar." Gradually the word acquired the sense of " rule, standard of accuracy "; therefore the books considered authoritative were termed " canonical." In general, evangelical scholars have not stressed the idea of canonicity in their discussions of inspiration. Presumably they assumed that the traditional Protestant canon determined the precise limits of plenary inspiration. Our purpose in this chapter is not to question this basic assumption but rather to examine the content of the accepted canon in order to determine the meaning that " plenary " must have if it is to be consistent with the phenomena of Scripture.

Plenary Inspiration and Duplicates

Although the King James Version does not indicate it, the book of The Psalms is actually a collection of five smaller books or compilations: Book 1 (Ps. 1-41), Book 2 (Ps. 42-72), Book 3 (Ps. 73-89), Book 4 (Ps. 90-106), and Book 5 (Ps. 107-150). These books are noted in the American Standard, Revised Standard, and Berkeley Versions. The Revised Standard Version also indicates, by footnotes, portions or whole psalms that are repeated elsewhere. For example, Ps. 14 is the same as Ps. 53. Both begin, "The fool says in his heart, 'There is no God.'"

While most scholars who hold to plenary inspiration recognize that much of what the prophets of God spoke has been lost and that even some of their writings may have perished as well, they attribute the existing canon directly to the providence of God. Only those writings which God decreed for us have been preserved. Did God determine that Ps. 14 should be repeated as Ps. 53? No doubt God inspired the psalmist, and in turn the psalm accredited itself to the hearts of the people, so that they felt like preserving it. But its occurrence twice in our collection of psalms is probably an accident of collection. Apparently when Book 2 was added to Book 1 the editor did not go through Book 2 deleting the similar passages. Scholars learn something about the transmission of Biblical books from comparing the two psalms (Ps. 14 tends to use "LORD," whereas Ps. 53 has "God"). From the standpoint of theological significance, however, what function does Ps. 53 serve in the Old Testament canon beyond that of Ps. 14?

There are a number of duplicate passages in Scripture. With the exception of Hezekiah's psalm (Isa. 38:9-20), chs. 36 to 39 in Isaiah are similar to II Kings 18:13 to 20:19. Moreover, Ps. 18 is repeated in II Sam., ch. 22; Ps. 40:13-17 = Ps. 70; Ps. 57:7-11 = Ps. 108:1-5; and Ps. 60:5-12 = Ps. 108:6-13. Most of these duplicates occurred in the process of compilation, yet the stress that inerrancy places on every word of the canon makes it necessary to attribute the duplicates to God's providence. Inasmuch as there are many portions of Scripture with greater theological significance (for example, Isa., ch. 53), one wonders why God did not have such passages repeated if it was his intention to teach redemptive truths through repetition.

Plenary Inspiration and Trivialities

According to the seventeenth-century Lutheran theologians, Scripture has no trivialities (*levicula*). In keeping with this view, as Preus comments, "Everything in Scripture pertains somehow to Christian doctrine."[1] Matters of very little consequence are related in some vital way to the total truth of Scripture because God has placed them there for an express purpose.

In Judg. 12:5-6 occurs the following narrative: "And the Gileadites took the fords of the Jordan against the Ephraimites. And when any of the fugitives of Ephraim said, 'Let me go over,' the men of Gilead said to him, 'Are you an Ephraimite?' When he said, 'No,' they said to him, 'Then say Shibboleth,' and he said 'Sibboleth,' for he could not pronounce it right; then they seized him and slew him at the fords of the Jordan. And there fell at that time forty-two thousand of the Ephraimites." This interesting little story has great value for the student of Semitic languages. In English the letter *s* is pronounced as a dental normally (for example, "sing"), but there are times when it has a palatal pronunciation (for example, "sure" and "sugar" where *s* = *sh*). Certain Semitic dialects and languages leveled through the *s sound,* so it was as difficult for these people to pronounce an *sh* as it is for a person of Germanic origin to say the English *th*. The scholar is delighted to find this linguistic example in Scripture, but from the standpoint of God's revelation the text could just as well have omitted the "Shibboleth" episode with vs. 5-6 reading as follows: "And the Gileadites took the fords of the Jordan against the Ephraimites. . . . And there fell at that time forty-two thousand of the Ephraimites."

The complete literature of Israel must have consisted of many other sources that somehow were lost or destroyed. The linguistic and archaelogical data incorporated in these documents would undoubtedly have been of great significance to the scholar, but it is questionable whether their disappearance constitutes any serious theological loss. On the other hand, is it not a bit questionable to attribute the "Shibboleth" story to the providential determination of God? Did God decree that this incident should be in the Old Testament canon? The Biblical writers were free to use any sources at hand; but in the case of certain individuals, information was so scarce that the writers included material which has little, if any, bearing on God's purpose in recording his revelation to man.

The case of Ibzan in Judg. 12:8-10 is quite illustrative: "After him Ibzan of Bethlehem judged Israel. He had thirty sons; and thirty daughters he gave in marriage outside his clan, and thirty daughters he brought in from outside for his sons. And he judged Israel seven years. Then Ibzan died, and was buried at Bethlehem." Surely if Ibzan judged Israel for seven years, he must have risen to his place of leadership on the basis of other attainments than that of marrying off his thirty daughters outside the clan and getting thirty girls imported as wives for his thirty sons. The compiler of The Book of Judges incorporated this information from some old source, but the text could just as well have read: "After him Ibzan of Bethlehem judged Israel. . . . And he judged Israel seven years. Then Ibzan died and was buried at Bethlehem." Because the information about Ibzan's children was in the source material at hand, are we duty-bound to find some providential purpose for its inclusion in Scripture?

Another example is found in Judg. 12:14, which informs us that Abdon "had forty sons and thirty grandsons, who rode on seventy asses; and he judged Israel eight years." This is all we know about the activities of Abdon. Are not God's ways exceedingly mysterious if, out of all the good things Abdon must have done, God decreed that we should have only this incident of Abdon's seventy sons and grandsons, each with his own means of transportation?

Inasmuch as revelation occurred in a historical context it is fitting that the historical framework play an important role in the record of that revelation. Notwithstanding some gaps and defects, the historical background enables us to understand the message of Scripture in a way that would never be possible otherwise. Inspiration had to do with the understanding of the historical record, not the inerrancy of every word incorporated from the sources.

Old Testament Canon and the Prophets

Philo and Josephus spoke of the Scriptures as being written by prophets, and in Matt. 26:56 Jesus is reported as saying, " But all this has taken place, that the scriptures of the prophets might be fulfilled." This information, along with the fact that a number of Old Testament books were clearly written by prophets, has led some conservative scholars to the theory that *all* the books were by prophets.[2] Solomon was a prophet, so it is reasoned, because God spoke to him in dreams on at least two occasions. Ecclesiastes, Song of Solomon, and Proverbs are to be classified as prophetic literature because they derive from Solomon. Judges, Ruth, Chronicles, Ezra, Nehemiah, Esther, and Job are considered as prophetic literature because there is no evidence that the authors of these books were not prophets. But does this easy answer not overlook some pertinent Biblical and non-Biblical data? New evidence supports the traditional claim that Ezra was the Chronicler, but Ezra 7:6 describes him as being " a scribe skilled in the law of Moses." Verse 10 says, " For Ezra had set his heart to study the law of the Lord, and to do it, and to teach his statutes and ordinances in Israel." The following verse describes him as " the priest, the scribe, learned in matters of the commandments of the Lord and his statutes in Israel." Nehemiah 8:9 refers to " Ezra the priest and scribe." There is no Biblical evidence that his contemporaries considered him a prophet.

His fame as a scribe is pictured in the apocryphal book known as Second Esdras (Fourth Ezra). Because God's revelation to man has perished, Ezra prays to God for inspiration to restore the Scriptures. Chapter 14:21-22 reads as follows: " For thy Law is burnt; and so no man knows the things which have been done by thee, or the works that shall be done. If then, I have found favor before thee, send into me the Holy Spirit, that I may write all that has happened in the world since the beginning, even the things which were written in thy Law, in order that men may be able to find the path, and that they who would live at the last may live." [3]

The story is completed in vs. 37-46: "So I took the five men as he had commanded me, and we went forth *into the field* and remained there. And it came to pass on the morrow that, lo! a voice called me, saying: Ezra, open thy mouth and drink what I give thee to drink! Then I opened my mouth, and lo! there was reached unto me a full cup, which was full as it were with water, but the colour of it was like fire. And I took it and drank; and when I had drunk, my heart poured forth understanding, wisdom grew in my breast, and my spirit retained its memory: and my mouth opened, and was no more shut. And the Most High gave understanding unto the five men, and they wrote what was dictated in order, in characters which they knew not. And so they sat forty days. They wrote in the day-time and at night did eat bread; but as for me, I spake in the day, and at night was not silent. So in forty days were written ninety-four books. And it came to pass when the forty days were fulfilled, that the Most High spake unto me saying: The twenty-four books that thou has written publish, that the worthy and unworthy may read (therein): but the seventy last thou shalt keep, to deliver them to the wise among thy people." [4]

The reference to twenty-four books is the ancient counting of the thirty-nine books in our present Old Testament (for example, the twelve Minor Prophets were considered one book). The seventy books were the apocryphal writings, which contained such deep wisdom only the very wise should read them. The story in its present form is clearly fictional, but there must have been some kernel of truth back of it. Perhaps Ezra played some important part in formalizing the Old Testament canon. At any rate, tradition does not recognize Ezra as a prophet any more than Scripture does.

If there is objection to Ezra as being the Chronicler, there can hardly be any doubt that he wrote the book which bears his name. Nehemiah also must have been largely responsible for the book that bears his name. But he is known as the "cupbearer to the king" in Persia, and "the governor" in Judah. Never is he recognized as a prophet.

Furthermore, Prov. 25:1 reads, "These also are proverbs of Solomon which the men of Hezekiah king of Judah copied." The editor who added this heading makes no reference to the "men of Hezekiah" as being prophets engaged in compilation of Scripture. Proverbs 22:17 reads, "Incline your ear, and hear the words of the wise," and ch. 24:23 states, "These also are sayings of the wise." These references are to other wise men than Solomon. Jeremiah 18:18 speaks of "counsel from the wise," and Ezek. 7:26 mentions "counsel from the elders." In other words, there was a clear concept of God revealing himself through some men other than the prophets. Chapter 30 in Proverbs is attributed to Agur, son of Jakeh of Massa. Massa is an Arabian tribe mentioned in Gen. 25:14, but that is all we know of the place name. Agur was probably no Israelite and less likely a prophet. Chapter 31 of Proverbs is attributed to Lemuel, king of Massa — words that his mother taught him. Was she a prophetess?

The Book of Ruth was passed on orally for a long period before it was put into written form. It is exceedingly doubtful that the prophets had a significant part in its oral transmission or its recording. It is just as doubtful that Esther or Job was written by the prophetic tradition. In the light of all this evidence, much of it from the Biblical text itself, is one warranted in ascribing all the Old Testament canon to the prophetic tradition?

Plenary Inspiration and The Book of Esther

Over and above the difficulties that are caused by duplicates, trivialities, and nonprophetic writings, there are some books that are on the edge of the canonical limits. Esther is one of these books. It purports to tell of God's vindication of the Jews in

Shushan (the capital city of the Persian Empire, known more commonly as Susa) during the reign of Ahasuerus (Xerxes), 486–465 B.C. Archaeology has not confirmed any of the events of Esther, but the book reflects Persian history and customs, and it is filled with Persian loan words. Oddly enough the name of God never appears in the book. God is certainly implicit in the whole story and numerous reasons have been given to account for the omission of the name. Later additions were made, apparently to correct this oversight, but these are considered apocryphal and do not appear in the regular Old Testament canon.

While most of the rabbis quoted in the Babylonian Talmud with respect to The Book of Esther believed that it was "composed [literally, "said"] under the inspiration of the Holy Spirit,"[5] some declared that the scroll of Esther "does not make the hands unclean."[6] The implication is that Esther did not share the unquestioned authority and canonical status of the Torah or the Prophets. These books, because of their holy character, "defiled the hands" of the readers.

In all likelihood the primary reason for Esther's being in the Hebrew canon was to show the origin of the Feast of Purim (first noted in II Macc. 15:36 as the day of Mordecai). The feast has always been, and continues to be, one of the most joyous of all the Jewish festivals. Raba, one of the Talmudic sages, gave the classical description for celebrating the feast when he said, "It is the duty of a man to mellow himself [with wine] on Purim until he cannot tell the difference between 'cursed be Haman' and 'blessed be Mordecai.'"[7]

In Christian circles Purim was not recognized as a legitimate festival of the church calendar, and so the explanation of the feast's origin ceased to have real relevance for Christians. In fact, at one time the Syrian Christians omitted The Book of Esther from their Syriac Old Testament. As a general rule today, however, Christians accept the canonicity of Esther, but they do so largely because the book shows God's providential care for his dispersed, persecuted people. Yet the fact of God's providential care is taught quite clearly in the books of Jeremiah and Ezekiel. Did God actually include The Book of Esther in the canon for this purpose, or is this an afterthought of Christians to justify the present Old Testament canon? The primary reason for Esther's inclusion has become a dead issue for Christians, and evidently the book did not occupy a very important place in the thinking of the New Testament writers, because it is never quoted in the New Testament. Is it really necessary, therefore, to contend for the unique inspiration of every word of Esther?

Plenary Inspiration and The Song of Songs

The Song of Songs (known also as Canticles or The Song of Solomon) is attributed to Solomon. In general, critical scholarship has discounted this claim, but in recent years new evidence has indicated that the book could well have come from the age of Solomon. Love songs were popular in the ancient world and a book of love songs dating from about 1100 B.C. has been discovered. It consists of seven cantos or units which express alternately the sentiments of lovers who call each other "brother" and "sister." Lovesickness plays an important part in the song. In Song of Songs we find the expression, "I am sick with love" (chs. 2:5; 5:8) and in ch. 5:1 the girl is addressed "my sister, my bride." In ch. 5:2 she is called "my sister, my love," while in ch. 8:1 she wishes that her lover "were like a brother to me."

It is the content, however, not the authorship, which is the basic problem relating to inspiration. Human love is expressed in such a frank, open manner that the book has been used sparingly for preaching and public reading. As a general rule Jews have allegorized the book in terms of God's love for Israel, and most Christians have followed suit by interpreting it as Christ's love for the church. This, to most people, was the only interpretation that would justify the book's being in the canon. In fact, Theodore of Mopsuestia was condemned by the Second Council of Constantinople (A.D. 533) because he thought the book was a mere song of human love that Solomon wrote for his marriage to Pharaoh's daughter.

Neither Jesus nor the New Testament writers find occasion to quote The Song of Songs. If the book was intended by God as a type or foreshadow of Christ and his love for the church, it is very odd that neither Jesus nor the apostles make mention of this fact. One factor that may have contributed to the book's inclusion in the canon is that the love song was a part of the great literature of other groups in the Orient and in like manner Solomon's love song became a part of Israel's collection of great literature. But whether literal truth or allegory, the most obvious reason for the book's place in the canon is the name of Solomon. The Song had its place in the age of Solomon and the following years, but it has long since ceased to serve its original function. Are we, then, to contend for the unique inspiration of its every word?

Plenary Inspiration and Ecclesiastes

The title Ecclesiastes derives from the Greek translation of the Hebrew word *qoheleth,* meaning "preacher." The Preacher identifies himself as "the son of David, king in Jerusalem" (ch. 1:1). Up to the Reformation, both Jews and Christians traditionally attributed the book to Solomon. Luther seems to have been the first Christian scholar to deny the Solomonic authorship. Since his time it has become increasingly apparent that the book is one of the latest compositions in the Old Testament canon. While early portions of the Old Testament tended to acquire some different linguistic features and editorial insertions later on during the process of transmission, they retained many aspects indicative of their antiquity. In the case of Ecclesiastes, however, both the language and the content witness against Solomonic authorship.

In recent years there has been considerable debate among conservative scholars over the date and authorship of Ecclesiastes. Some frankly admit that the author lived after the exile and placed his words in the mouth of Solomon as a literary device.[8]

Others conclude that ch. 1:1 clearly attributes the book to Solomon and so they maintain the Solomonic authorship. To do otherwise would be an admission that Ecclesiastes is in the category of the apocryphal book The Wisdom of Solomon.[9] The former view counters with the assertion that the Preacher in v. 1 is not Solomon and the original readers of the book would never have interpreted the literary device in this way.[10]

It is very charitable to speak of the unambiguous literary character of the book and to affirm that it would have deceived none of its original readers, but what is the *historical* justification for such a view? In ch. 1:12 the text reads, "I the Preacher have been [was] king over Israel in Jerusalem." Apparently, the author was not on the throne at this time, but Solomon, according to the historical books, reigned until his death. To get around this contradiction, the Jewish sages concluded that Solomon's sin resulted in the loss of his regal powers.

In section 20b of the unit "Sanhedrin" in the Babylonian Talmud there is an extended passage dealing with the problem of Solomon's gradually restricted authority. The rabbis note (quoting Eccl. 1:12) that at first Solomon was king over all Israel, then (quoting ch. 1:1) they observe that his authority extended only over Jerusalem. They believed that Solomon, becoming like a commoner, was finally stripped of all power, except his own staff. Was Solomon ever restored to power? Some of the rabbinical authorities thought so, but others said he remained a commoner forever.

Further discussion of Ecclesiastes occurs in section 68b of unit "Gittin." One of the main points in this section is to account for the Solomonic authorship of Ecclesiastes. It is difficult to say how far back these ideas go into Jewish history, but one thing is clear: tradition knows of no time when the Solomonic authorship was doubted.

The book was questioned, but not on grounds of authorship. The Talmud notes: "The Sages wished to hide the book of Ecclesiastes, because its words are self-contradictory; yet why did they not hide it? Because its beginning is religious teaching and its end is religious teaching."[11] From start to finish, the Talmudic discussion of Ecclesiastes assumes Solomonic authorship. Christian tradition followed suit, apparently, although the New Testament writers found no occasion to quote from the book.

On what grounds, then, can one declare that none of the original readers were deceived? At best it is an assumption, and even if one grants its validity, it was not long before tradition attributed Ecclesiastes to Solomon. It is this fact which accounts for the book's being in the canon.

While some of the conservative scholars are willing to deny the Solomonic authorship, they usually date the book prior to 400 B.C. This also is to protect the book because traditionally the canon has been considered as having been completed by 400 B.C., the time, according to later Jewish tradition, that the spirit of prophecy departed from Israel. However, the linguistic features of the book along with evidence from fragments of Ecclesiastes found at Qumrân point to the third century B.C. as the date of composition. Thus we are faced with the possibility that a canonical book was composed after 400 by someone putting his message in the mouth of Solomon, yet without actually using his name.

About 180 B.C. a certain Jesus, the son of Sira(ch), a Jerusalem Jew, composed a book in Hebrew. He frankly gave his name and as a result his teachings, although quite popular, were never granted canonical status by the Jews. However, the book, known as the wisdom of Sirach, was read a great deal by the Christian church, and for this reason it acquired the title Ecclesiasticus, "Church Book." In terms of theological relevance and impact on Judaism and Christianity, the book of Ecclesiasticus has had far more influence than has the canonical book Ecclesiastes. Accordingly, the author who uses a literary device, leaving the impression of Solomonic authorship (without actually employing the name), has his book included in the canon, while the author who has much to say, but honestly names himself, finds his work excluded from the canon.

Plenary Inspiration and the Old Testament

After this rather lengthy discussion of the Old Testament canon it should be apparent that the books of the Old Testament range from works of unquestioned authority and revelational content to those of questionable authority and rather insignificant value. Some portions of the apocryphal books appear to have greater worth than some sections of the canonical books, but somewhere a line had to be drawn. Considering books as a whole (not as units or verses), the Jewish community made the decision. It is implicit that Jesus accepted the Hebrew canon (which rejected the apocryphal books), but there is no evidence in the New Testament to indicate what his opinion was regarding some of the canonical books, because he neither quoted them nor alluded to them. For practical reasons, canonical limits had to be set, but does this mean that every word within these limits is uniquely inspired of God, while every word outside the canon is not inspired?

John Bunyan, with many other great Christians both past and present, would answer, "No!" In his *Grace Abounding* he relates how, in a period of great despondency, the following words came to mind: "Look at the generations of old and see: did ever any trust in the Lord and was confounded?" He searched the Bible for these comforting words, but they were not to be found. He asked his Christian friends concerning the words, but they too could not identify the source. About a year later he found the statement in Ecclus. 2:10. "This at first," writes Bunyan, "did somewhat daunt me, because it was not in those texts that we call holy and canonical; yet as this sentence was the sum and substance of many of the promises, it was my duty to take the comfort of it. And I bless God for that word, for it was of good to me. That word doth still ofttimes shine before my face." Bunyan was wise enough to see that God was the source of all redemptive, moral truth, whether that truth was found in canonical or apocryphal books.

Plenary Inspiration and the New Testament

The traditional criterion for a canonical New Testament book has been apostolic authorship; that is, every book was written by an apostle or one closely associated with him (for example, Mark with Peter, and Luke with Paul). Some have claimed, on the other hand, that the original basis for canonicity was not apostolic authorship but apostolic authority which imposed (as law) on the churches any book that it deemed worthy, whether the book was written by an apostle or not.[12]

Inasmuch as every New Testament book supposedly has the imprimatur of the apostles, the complete accuracy of every word of the canon is assured. Any conclusion, therefore, that runs counter to a Biblical affirmation is inconsistent with the true doctrine of inspiration regardless of the apparent evidence supporting it.

But how does the book of Jude, for example, fit in with this theory? The book purports to have been composed by Jude, the brother of James (leader of the church at Jerusalem and half-brother of Jesus). The book was one of the last to be accepted into the canon because its authorship and validity were disputed. Yet this doubt would hardly have been an issue if Peter, John, or Paul had authorized the book and imposed it on the early church.

Moreover, according to the doctrine of plenary inspiration every word of Jude is inspired. But Jude, as we have seen, quotes the book of Enoch in the belief that he is quoting Enoch the pre-Flood patriarch. By definition the quoted words are inspired because they are supposedly from an authoritative, God-given source and they actually occur within New Testament canonical limits.

Some scholars in the past have gone so far as to say that the verse quoted from Enoch was inspired, while the rest of Enoch was not. Jude, so they claim, is not sanctioning the book of Enoch any more than Paul sanctions the words of Aratus, Menander, and Epimenides, the Greek poets whom he quotes in

Acts 17:28; I Cor. 15:33; Titus 1:12. There is, however, a real difference between the two situations. Paul refers to the statements of the Greek poets because they accord with what he already knows to be true, but he does not profess to quote them as Scripture. These true statements serve as a point of contact with his hearers or readers. Jude, on the other hand, says, "Enoch in the seventh generation from Adam prophesied saying, . . ." Enoch is no pagan poet — he is a prophet of God whose prophecy is coming true in Jude's own day.

Jude also refers to other parts of Enoch. Verse 6 reads, "And the angels that did not keep their own position but left their proper dwelling have been kept by him in eternal chains in the nether gloom until the judgment of the great day." This is not a quotation but a summary of the point of view expressed in chs. 6 to 16 of Enoch. We may infer, therefore, that aside from ch. 1:9, Jude considered portions of Enoch as also being authoritative. We have also noted Jude's dependence on the apocryphal book The Assumption of Moses. What are we to make of all these affirmations by Jude? Would it not be preferable to acknowledge the facts and claim inspiration for Jude on the basis of the truths found in the book? In spite of the difficulties, this little book of twenty-five verses has an authoritative ring which sets it apart from the New Testament apocryphal books and from the writings of the early church fathers.

John Henry Newman put the whole matter of the canon very well when he wrote: "Providence never acts with harsh transitions, one thing melts into another. Day melts into night, summer into winter. So it is with His inspired Word. What is *divine* gradually resolves into what is human. Yet, as nevertheless summer and winter have for practical purposes a line of division, as St. Paul dissuaded the shipmen from sailing because the fast was already past and sailing dangerous, so we too for practical purposes are obliged to draw a line and say what is safe and sure to take as a canon for our faith, and what we cannot be sure will not mislead us. Without therefore, far from it, denying that God's supernatural hand is in the Apocrypha, yet knowing that it was not included in that Canon which Christ sanctions, and that his church has not spoken so clearly on the subject as to overcome the positive face of the argument deductible from this silence, therefore we do not see our way clear to receive it as canonical."[18]

The Protestant canon of the Bible is well able to achieve God's purpose in revealing himself to mankind. There is a shading off at the fringes of Scripture, but the sufficiency of the redemptive message is not marred thereby. For this reason we need not attempt to justify every word within the canon.

7: *Tradition and Inspiration*

Our discussion thus far has considered the teaching and phenomena of Scripture under various topics that constitute the doctrine of inspiration. It is fitting now to approach the problem from the history of doctrine. There have been a number of outstanding individuals in the history of the church who were influential in the development of the doctrine of inspiration. If these Christian leaders, representing a wide range of time, geographical area, cultural background, and psychological temperament, set forth a consistent view of inspiration, we would be obligated to give great weight to their point of view.[1] Accordingly, our purpose in this study will be to note the emphases of these men, both in theory and in practice, in order to determine (1) the extent to which they agree, and (2) the extent of precise detail inherent in their formulations. In brief, we are concerned to learn whether or not there has been a classic doctrine of inspiration, and if so, what its characteristics are.

Inasmuch as the early church grew out of Judaism, it is necessary that we begin our survey with the doctrine of inspiration as set forth by one of the most influential Jews.

Philo

The Jewish philosopher Philo (about 20 B.C. to A.D. 50) from Alexandria, Egypt, had an extraordinary influence on Christian as well as Jewish thought. Exclusive of books which may have been lost, and those which have been spuriously attributed to him, Philo wrote thirty-eight different works. Four deal with special problems of philosophy, while three tell of current Jewish events in Alexandria. The remaining thirty-one deal primarily with the Torah or Pentateuch (Genesis through Deuteronomy), being either running commentary on the text or discussions of topics found therein.

Philo believed that there were three sources of prophecy or revelation: (1) the Voice of God, (2) the Divine Spirit, and (3) angels. All three means of revelation are divine, even though angels can reveal to a non-Jew. The Divine Spirit reveals in Scripture, but this same Spirit can also give prophecy to a non-Jew of moral character. The Voice of God, however, is direct prophecy that occurs only in the Scripture given to the Jews.

But Philo's doctrine of inspiration must be evaluated in the light of other views that he held. The basic text for his theological writings was the Septuagint. Concerning the translators of this version, Philo wrote, "Reflecting how great an undertaking it was to make a full version of the laws given by the Voice of God, where they could not add or take away or transfer anything, but must keep the original form and shape, they proceeded to look for the most open and unoccupied spot in the neighborhood outside the city."[2] Having decided upon the island of Pharos, in the harbor of Alexandria, Egypt, the translators began their task, which Philo describes as follows: "Sitting here in seclusion with none present save the elements of nature, earth, water, air, heaven, the genesis of which was to be the first theme of their sacred revelation, for the laws begin with the story of the world's creation, they became as it were possessed, and, under inspiration, wrote, not each several scribe something different, but the same word for word, as though dictated to each by an invisible prompter."[3]

This statement shows that for Philo the Septuagint was as divinely inspired and authoritative as the Hebrew Scriptures. The translators, being "prophets and priests" who had the "spirit of Moses," made an absolutely accurate translation, and the finished product of each of the seventy-two scribes agreed identically, word for word, "as though dictated to each by an invisible prompter." Here in its clearest terms is the dictation theory of inspiration applied to the translation of the Septuagint.

Some Christians are convinced that the New Testament writers agreed with Philo in considering the Old Testament Scriptures as the "oracles of God," but they reject, on the other hand, any implications that the New Testament writers also followed Philo in his view of the Septuagint. One wonders, however, whether anyone can legitimately accept a certain facet of Philo's teaching while rejecting another aspect of his formulation which is equally basic to his overall view of inspiration.

Another aspect of Philo's thinking that has some bearing on his doctrine of inspiration is his manner of interpreting the Old Testament. He assumes that Scripture has two meanings: (1) the literal, obvious meaning, and (2) the underlying meaning, described most often by the term "allegory." "To allegorize," therefore, was to interpret the Scriptures in accordance with the hidden meaning. Only talented people with training and moral character were qualified for instruction in this method. With regard to Philo's use of these two methods of interpretation Harry A. Wolfson notes: "Everything in Scripture, from names, dates, and numbers to the narration of historical events or the prescription of rules for human conduct, is to him subject to allegorical interpretation. But as for the literal method, it is to be used, according to him, with certain reservations. One general rule laid down by Philo is that no anthropomorphic expression about God is to be taken literally. As proof text for this general rule he quotes the verse 'God is not as man,' which is taken by him to contain the general principle that God is not to be likened to anything perceptible by the senses."[4] Thus, in the Genesis account "it is quite foolish to think that the world was created in six days or in a space of time at all," because *six* is "not a quantity of days, but a perfect number," indicating that creation took place in a certain plan and order.[5]

The only time the literal meaning of historical events must be rejected, according to Philo, is whenever such an interpretation compels the reader to admit anything base or unworthy of the inspired words of God. The story in Gen. 37:13-14 of Jacob sending Joseph to see how his brothers and the flocks were faring cannot be accepted literally by any sensible person, for "is it likely that Jacob, who had the wealth of a king, was so badly off for household servants or attendants as to send a son out abroad to bring word about his other children, whether they are in good health, and about the cattle to boot?"[6] Nevertheless, Philo would not doubt that Joseph, for some other reason, went to see his brothers and was sold by them. Wolfson comments: "All these statements merely show that by the allegorical method Philo found it possible to explain away any narration of incident in Scripture that seemed to him to run counter to reason or expectation or to have some similarity with Greek myths, without necessarily impugning the historicity of the essential basic fact of the story."[7] But concern for the essential facts of the Bible does not involve precision of *all* details, so is not Philo in *practice,* then, negating some aspects of his *theory* of inspiration?

Early Church Fathers

Justin Martyr (about A.D. 100–165), an early defender of Christianity, wrote a book which he entitled Apology (meaning "Defense"). In this work, as well as in his other writings, appear numerous statements indicating his view of inspiration. Concerning the prophets, he affirms: "But when you hear the utterances of the prophets spoken as it were personally, you must not suppose that they are spoken by the inspired themselves, but by the Divine Word who moves them. . . . For they do not present to you artful discourses . . . but use with simplicity the words and expressions which offer themselves, and declare to you whatever the Holy Ghost, who descended upon them, chose to teach through them to those who are desirous to learn the true religion."[8] Thus, while stressing the activity of the Holy Spirit, Justin did not deny the part played by the human instrument.

Probably the most extreme view of inspiration held by any of the church fathers was that proposed by Athenagoras. He was unknown to the church fathers of the third and fourth centuries, and little is known of his life. Apparently Athenagoras, an Athenian philosopher, became a convert to Christianity while studying Scripture in an attempt to refute it. Later he wrote an apology for the Christians, addressing it (about A.D. 177) to the Roman emperor Marcus Aurelius and his son Commodus. He said that the prophets "lifted in ecstasy above the natural operations of their minds by the impulses of the Divine Spirit, uttered the things with which they were inspired, the Spirit making use of them as a flute player breathes into a flute."[9] It would appear that Athenagoras held to a strict *dictation* view of inspiration, but it is difficult to show that he meant precisely the same thing as we do by the term "dictation."

The greatest of the early church fathers was undoubtedly Irenaeus (about A.D. 125–202). He was reared at Smyrna in Asia Minor. In 177, while a missionary in Gaul, he was appointed Bishop of Lyons. Considering his greatest task to be an opponent of Gnostic rationalism, he wrote Five Books Against Heresies, throughout which are scattered numerous statements describing his view of Scripture.

The inspiration of the Scriptures, according to Irenaeus, involved both the inspired man and the inspiration of the Spirit, making the writings the words of God. In theory, therefore, he denied the dictation view of Scripture, yet at the same time he always considered the inspiration of the book as transcending that of the man. The book, however, was the Septuagint, since Irenaeus spoke Greek, and, like Philo, he considered the LXX just as inspired and authoritative as the Hebrew text.

There are indications that Irenaeus rebelled against the allegorical type of interpretation which was so popular with the Christians and Gnostics at Alexandria. He was still a child of his age, however, and though holding to the literal method in theory, he often took great liberties with his own rule. Balaam's ass was a type of Christ, the three (?) spies who came to Rahab represented the Trinity, Gideon's fleece was a type of Israel, the Last Supper and Gethsemane were types of the descent into hell, and the good Samaritan was a type of the work of the Holy Spirit. Notwithstanding these interpretive lapses, Irenaeus has been considered by some scholars as holding to the verbal plenary view of inspiration.[10] But how can this be when he believed in the inspiration of the Septuagint? As observed previously, the modern interpretation of verbal plenary inspiration denies that any translation, even the LXX, can be inspired.

Tertullian (about A.D. 150–230), the fiery, devout Christian from Carthage, North Africa, expressed his view of inspiration as follows: "From the beginning He sent into the world men who, because of their innocence and righteousness, were worthy to know God and to make Him known to others. These men He filled with the Holy Spirit, that they might teach that there is but one God who made the universe and formed man from the earth."[11] He did not hesitate, therefore, to call the Scriptures the "writings of God" or the "words of God." Yet this general use of language should not be pushed too far. Furthermore, since Scripture (as defined by Tertullian) meant a Latin translation of the Bible, one cannot actually attribute the present-day interpretation of verbal plenary inspiration to him either.

Origen (about A.D. 185–254), the most scholarly of the early church fathers, studied under Clement of Alexandria, and later became the leading teacher of the Alexandrian School. Inasmuch as Clement and Origen were in Alexandria, the shadow of Philo was bound to fall across both of them. Clement claimed there was an allegorical meaning throughout the entire Bible, and Origen, in principle, followed in his teacher's footsteps. All of Scripture, according to Origen, came to be recorded through the power of the Holy Spirit, so he could declare: "Small wonder if every word spoken by the prophets produced the proper effect of a word. Nay, I hold that every wonderful letter written in the oracles of God has its effects. There is not one jot or one tittle written in Scripture which, for those who know how to use the power of the Scriptures, does not effect its proper work." [12]

As the first great scholar to deal with the problem of the New Testament text, Origen knew there were difficulties in the various wordings of the Greek manuscripts available to him, but he felt that all of them could be overcome eventually with the allegorical method. Where the Greek text was clear, he admitted problems in connection with the literal meaning. He confessed: "And in many other instances, if a man carefully examines the Gospels with discrepancies of the narrative in view, . . . bewilderment will fall upon him, and either, abandoning all attempt to give the Gospels their real authority, he will arbitrarily adhere to one of them, not having courage to reject entirely his faith in our Lord; or else he must accept the four with the admission that their truth lies not in their outward and visible features." [13] It is unlikely that this statement and Origen's allegorical method of defending the absolute truthfulness of Scripture conform precisely to the doctrine of verbal plenary inspiration as defined today.

In summarizing the views of inspiration held by the early church fathers, B. F. Westcott (1825–1901) comments: "The unanimity of the early fathers in their views on Holy Scripture is the more remarkable when it is taken in connexion with the great differences of character and training and circumstances by which they were distinguished. In the midst of errors of judgment and errors of detail they maintain firmly with one consent the great principles which invest the Bible with an interest most special and most universal, with the characteristics of the most vivid individuality and of the most varied application. They teach us that inspiration is an operation of the Holy Spirit acting *through* men, according to the laws of their constitution, which is not neutralized by his influence, but adopted as a vehicle for the full expression of the divine message." [14] Finally, Westcott affirms: "It is possible that objections, more or less serious, may be urged against various parts of the doctrine, but it cannot, I think, be denied that as a whole it lays open a view of the Bible which vindicates with the greatest clearness and consistency the claims which it makes to be considered as one harmonious message of GOD, spoken *in many parts and many manners* by men and to men — the distinct lessons of individual ages reaching from one time to all time."[15]

Westcott was not explicit as to the meaning of "full expression," but it would appear that he was referring to Scripture as a statement of God's redemptive purpose and activity which is sufficiently complete to achieve the desired goal with respect to mankind. Since Westcott was not ignorant of the variation within Scripture, his reference to "one harmonious message of God" was most likely an allusion to the essential unity of God's redemptive message in both the Old and New Testaments.

Accordingly, Westcott was convinced that these early church fathers saw clearly the great principles which are in the Bible and that their doctrine "as a whole" vindicates the claims which Scripture makes for itself. At the same time, however, he makes it equally clear that beyond the general truths of their formulations there are errors of judgment and detail which are subject to more or less serious objection. This dual estimate evidences Westcott's insight and objectivity, and there is little reason to question the validity of his conclusions.

Later Church Fathers

Two fathers are worthy of note in the next period of church history: Jerome (347–420), the famous scholar who made the Latin translation of the Bible known later as the Latin Vulgate, and Augustine (354–430), the remarkable Bishop of Hippo in North Africa. The two were of extremely different temperaments and as a result they approached Scripture with exceedingly divergent points of view. At the risk of oversimplifying matters, E. Harris Harbison contrasts the two men as follows: "Jerome was a philologist, a lover of words and language;

Augustine, a philosopher, a lover of ideas. . . . For over twenty years (394–416) the two argued over scriptural interpretation by correspondence across half the Mediterranean. Augustine believed that the *Septuagint* was an inspired translation of the Old Testament into Greek, of equal authority with the Hebrew, if not greater. Jerome based himself upon philological analysis of the Hebrew. Augustine was particularly troubled by Jerome's insinuation that St. Paul was, on one occasion at least, a liar. Jerome was not one to take such criticism lying down, of course, and the controversy was boiling merrily when Jerome finally decided that it was making a bad impression on heretics and called it off. 'I have decided to love you,' he wrote Augustine. Jerome was a great scholar who was a Christian; Augustine was a great Christian who left an indelible mark on scholarship." [16]

In a letter to Jerome dating from about A.D. 405, Augustine wrote, "For, I admit to your charity that it is from those books alone of the Scriptures, which are now called canonical, that I have learned to pay them such honor and respect as to believe most firmly that not one of their authors has erred in writing anything at all." [17] This quotation appears to be a clear reference to the inerrancy of the original writings, but such an interpretation fails to recognize that Augustine read Scripture in a Latin translation made from the Septuagint. This fact, in conjunction with Augustine's belief in the inspiration of the Septuagint, makes it difficult to read back into Augustine's declaration the modern interpretation of verbal plenary inspiration. This conclusion is supported by the fact that those who believe in the inerrancy of the original writings have sided with Jerome in rejecting Augustine's view of the Septuagint while at the same time holding to Augustine's formulation of inspiration.

In common with most of his predecessors, Augustine's doctrine of inspiration must also be viewed in the light of his use of the allegorical method. He admitted frankly that this was a means of solving the difficult problems of the Old Testament. The "sun which comes forth like a bridegroom leaving his chamber" (Ps. 19:4-5) was for Augustine a reference to Christ's emergence from the Virgin's womb. He prided himself in the belief that he had seen hidden meanings in the Old Testament which had not been observed by the New Testament writers.

One of Augustine's pet subjects was numerics or numerology, and he was not to be outdone by any of his predecessors. An extreme illustration is his attempt to find a sacred meaning for the number 50, which was associated with Pentecost. He suggested taking 50 three times (for the Father, Son, and Holy Spirit) and adding three (the number in the Trinity), making a total of 153. Since this total is the same as the number of fish taken after the resurrection of the Lord, it indicates the special sanctity of the number 50. "And so," Augustine continues, "certain mysteries of comparison are expressed in the Sacred Books in many other numbers and arrangements of numbers, which are hidden from readers because of their ignorance of numbers."[18] This emphasis on numerics was actually a reversion, however, because Irenaeus had pointed out, two centuries earlier, the folly of such an approach to Scripture.

Of all the church fathers, Augustine's formulation comes the closest to expressing the doctrine of inerrancy, but his theory appears to be vitiated in practice both by dependence on allegorical and numerological interpretations of Scripture and by belief in the inspiration of the Septuagint.

The Reformation

For over a thousand years after Jerome and Augustine there was little change in the formulation of the doctrine of inspiration; we are justified, therefore, in moving on to the towering figures of the Reformation, Martin Luther (1483–1546) and John Calvin (1509–1564). Since both of these men wrote so much over such a long period of time and from so many different theological contexts, it is difficult to formulate clearly from their works their doctrines of inspiration.

In rejecting the authority of the pope, Luther was compelled to place great emphasis on the authority of Scripture. Since he assigned the entire Scriptures to the Holy Spirit, he considered them the Word of the most exalted God, not the word of man. Luther said that the so-called trivial things in the Bible were divinely inspired, and in one context declared that the Scriptures had never erred.

On the basis of these and similar ideas expressed in Luther's writings, certain scholars are convinced of Luther's belief in the inerrancy of Scripture. On the contrary, other twentieth-century theologians are convinced that Luther broke with the traditional view of inspiration. The ground for this view is Luther's consistent appeal to Christ as the essence of the gospel. Using this criterion, Luther is bold enough to call the book of James, where Christ is seldom mentioned, a very "strawy epistle." With this facet of Luther's thinking as their basis, these scholars today affirm that whenever Luther uses the expression "Word of God" he is not thinking about the Scriptures, the written word, but Christ, the Living Word of God. If this is true, one is perplexed by Luther's explicit declaration in another context: "No other doctrine should be proclaimed in the church than the pure Word of God, that is, the Holy Scriptures."[19] Apparently this diversity of interpretation with respect to Luther's writings stems from his concern to protect both the divine and the human aspects of Scripture.

Whereas Luther was of a more practical turn of mind, his younger contemporary, John Calvin, possessed an amazingly systematic, orderly mind which produced at the early age of twenty-six the *Institutes of the Christian Religion*. In many respects his views on inspiration are more clear-cut than Luther's, yet he also wrote much that is ambiguous in nature. While some interpreters of Calvin contend that not a single word can be taken as favoring a literal inspiration, others affirm that Calvin held to a verbal, inerrant view of inspiration.

This extreme diversity of interpretation results from two sets of data relating to Scripture. When speaking of the Bible as a whole, Calvin stresses its divine origin and authority. He affirms in many places that the writings of Scripture were dictated to the prophets and apostles by the Holy Spirit. But he does not mean mechanical dictation, because in other contexts he is strongly opposed to the concept that conceived of the Biblical writers as mere robots. The term "dictation" was for Calvin the means of declaring the divine aspect of Scripture.

Over against this general affirmation, however, must be placed the statements that Calvin made when dealing with the phenomena and teaching of the sacred text. After the Pharisees accused the disciples of desecrating the Sabbath, Jesus countered them with a reference to "the burnt offering of every sabbath" (Num. 28:10): "Or have you not read in the law how on the sabbath the priests in the temple profane the sabbath, and are guiltless?" (Matt. 12:5). At this point in his commentary Calvin claims that Jesus has accommodated himself to his hearers and so the statement is not "strictly accurate." In commenting on the disbelief of Thomas (John 20:25), Calvin notes again how human ignorance makes it necessary for God to accommodate himself to man's way of speaking. Calvin even suggests that at times God "stammers" in his attempt to communicate with his creatures.

The repetitions of I John 2:14 are "superfluous," according to Calvin. Although not doubting the meaning of the passage, he claims that "bitter jealousy and selfish ambition in your hearts" (James 3:14) is an "improper" way of speaking. Psalm 83:9 reads, "Do to them as thou didst to Midian, as to Sisera and Jabin at the river Kishon." Only the Canaanites Jabin and Sisera were defeated at the Kishon, and so Calvin acknowledges that the psalmist mingles two histories together. "Strict accuracy" would demand a revision of the sentence.

One of the most conspicuous examples of Calvin's paradoxical handling of Scripture is found in The Book of Jeremiah. He comments on ch. 1:2 that even though v. 1 refers to "the words of Jeremiah," God is really the author of Jeremiah's words. Yet in commenting on Jeremiah's bitter complaint against God (ch.

20:14-18), Calvin contends that a blind, insane impulse caused Jeremiah to utter these ungrateful, inconsiderate words which are directed against man as well as God. Was God the author of these impious words?

The ambiguity in the writings of Luther and Calvin stems, of course, from the complex nature of Scripture and its inspiration. They claimed repeatedly, as had their predecessors, that Scripture derived from God, thus it was God's written word. But in their attempt to refute the dictation view, such as expressed by Athenagoras, they also contended for the reality of man's part in the process. Where man's part was in danger of being denied or overlooked, Luther and Calvin were quick to correct the error. Yet, in contexts where the divine aspects of the Bible were at stake, both of them rallied to the defense of God's part in the recording of Scripture.

Prior to the period of the Reformation, no doctrinal statement on inspiration was ever formulated at the great councils convened by the church. Among the earliest creedal statements was the Belgic Confession of Faith (1561). Article VII of this formulation, drafted by Guido de Brès, refers to Scripture as "this infallible rule." Scholars in the Reformed tradition are still trying to determine what the statement meant to those who framed and adopted this confession of faith. The clue, according to some, is the preceding sentence, which characterizes man's ways and words as false and vain. God's words, on the contrary, are neither false nor vain. They never deceive and they will never fail or return empty. God's words will always accomplish the purpose for which they were given (Isa. 55:11). It is interesting to note that a Latin translation done in London rendered the original French text as "this most certain rule." This translation, which met with approval at the Synod of Dordt, raises the question as to what extent the concept of inerrancy was actually intended. In any case it points up the ambiguity that existed in the minds of Luther, Calvin, and all religious leaders of the sixteenth century. The doctrine of inspiration had not yet developed to the point where God's part and man's part in Scripture were considered simultaneously. This refinement in doctrine was to come later with the rise of the scientific method and the critical mind.

Post-Reformation

Whereas Luther and Calvin had some trying times in the sixteenth century, their troubles were not to be compared with those of the theologians in the seventeenth century. In this difficult period the Protestants had to defend themselves against the Counter-Reformation of the Roman Catholic Church as well as against the secularism and liberalism of the burgeoning scientific age. Moreover, from 1600 to 1700 Europe had only about seven years of peace, and the violent hatreds that were rampant throughout the Continent infested the Christian church as well.

One of the outstanding defenders of the faith in the seventeenth century was J. A. Quenstedt. The fame of his dogmatic theology won for him the nickname "Bookkeeper of Lutheran Orthodoxy." He formulated his doctrine of inspiration as follows: "The canonical Holy Scriptures in the original text are the infallible truth and are free from every error; in other words, in the canonical sacred Scriptures there is found no lie, no falsity, no error, not even the least, whether in subject matter or expressions, but in all things and all the details that are handed down in them, they are most certainly true, whether they pertain to doctrines or morals, to history or chronology, to topography or nomenclature. No ignorance, no thoughtlessness, no forgetfulness, no lapse of memory can and are to be ascribed to the amanuenses [scribes] of the Holy Ghost in their penning the Sacred Writings."[20] Although such exactitude of details would seem to approximate the mechanical dictation view of inspiration, the Biblical writers, according to Quenstedt, were not in a trance when the Holy Spirit spoke to them. Rather, they wrote cheerfully, willingly, and intelligently. Thus, instead of alleviating the problem, the systematic refinements of Quenstedt only served to heighten the ambiguity that was inherent in his predecessors.

While Quenstedt represented the followers of Luther, the Westminster Confession (1647) represented Calvin's adherents. Chapter I sets forth the doctrine relating to Holy Scripture. After listing the Protestant canon, Article II affirms that all these books were "given by inspiration of God to be the rule of faith and life." Article V speaks of the "entire perfection" and "infallible truth" of the Word of God. This would appear to argue for the inerrancy of Scripture, and yet Article II seems to restrict these qualities specifically to the areas of faith and life. For this reason the Westminster Confession has been commonly interpreted to mean that Scripture is "the infallible rule for faith and practice." Since the Bible does not claim to speak authoritatively in the realms of science, for example, one can allow for errors of fact in such areas.

With respect to the autographs and manuscript transmission, Article VIII states that the Old Testament in Hebrew and the New Testament in Greek were "immediately inspired by God." Scripture in the original languages is "authentical" because God by his "singular care and providence" kept the manuscripts "pure in all ages." The stress is on the authenticity and purity of the extant manuscripts in Hebrew and Greek. The original writings were "inspired by God," but it does not say that this inspiration was characterized by an inerrancy which was lost during the process of transmission. Language that can refer to copies of Scripture as being "pure" is most certainly not precise enough to be interpreted as intending explicit reference to inerrant autographs.

The failure of the sixteenth- and seventeenth-century theologians to understand the precise implications of their formulations is illustrated by their belief in the accuracy of the vowel points in the extant Hebrew manuscripts of the Old Testament. The Hebrew alphabet was, and is, composed of consonants. While some of these consonants were also used to indicate certain long vowels, Hebrew manuscripts did not indicate *all* of the vowels prior to about A.D. 600. It is impossible, of course, to speak without using vowels, so in learning to read the Hebrew Bible aloud, it was necessary to learn which vowels to supply. This *oral tra-*

dition, passed on from generation to generation, was undoubtedly the primary means for determining the vowel signs to be added to the manuscripts.

By about 1600 the validity of the vowel signs (known as " vowel points ") became a matter of dispute between the Jesuits and the Lutherans. The Jesuits denied their authenticity, while the Lutherans and almost all the other Protestant theologians contended for their accuracy. The battle raged even more furiously among the Reformed theologians, who carried on the ideas and work of John Calvin and Theodore Beza (1519–1605). During the years 1645–1653, Johann Buxtorf the younger carried on a violent dispute with Cappellus. Buxtorf's belief in the antiquity and divine authority of the vowel points was given public approval when the Swiss Reformed Churches incorporated his ideas into their new confession of faith, *Formula Consensus Helvetica,* and formally adopted it in 1675.

Although this extreme article of faith is rejected by the Reformed tradition today, it bears out the fact that all the creedal statements on inspiration formulated during the sixteenth and seventeenth centuries were precritical in nature and that they neither elaborated nor reconciled the divine and human elements of Scripture in any systematic way. This attitude was also true of John Wesley (1703–1791), the founder of Methodism. The Bible, for him, was God's Word, but it was mediated through human instrumentality. Thus, from Irenaeus in the second century up to the turn of the nineteenth century, the formulations of inspiration were essentially general affirmations of the divine and human aspects of Scripture. Nowhere were these two facets of the truth explicitly reconciled.

Modern Period

The most influential advocates of the verbal plenary view of inspiration during the nineteenth century were Louis Gaussen (1790–1863) of Geneva, Switzerland, and Benjamin B. Warfield (1851–1921) in the United States of America. Gaussen defined inspiration as "that inexplicable power which the Divine Spirit put forth of old on the authors of holy Scripture, in order to their guidance even in the employment of the words they used, and to preserve them alike from all error and from all omission."[21] To forestall any accusations of "mechanical dictation view" he discussed at great length the individuality of the sacred writers. Although admitting that he could not explain how the *full* activity of God and of man were possible at the same time in Scripture, Gaussen asserted, "There, all the words are man's; as there, too, all the words are God's."[22] Here, as with all his predecessors, Gaussen is endeavoring to protect God's part in Scripture along with man's. Notwithstanding this sincere attempt, however, one can hardly refrain from asking, How, in the light of scientific data concerning Scripture and its origin, can the Divine and human aspects of the Bible be pushed to the point where both function equally in every word?

Warfield's definition, still considered by many as the classic formulation, is as follows: "Inspiration is that extraordinary, supernatural influence (or, passively, the result of it,) exerted by the Holy Ghost on the writers of our Sacred Books, by which their words were rendered also the words of God, and, therefore, perfectly infallible."[23]

Twentieth-century restatements of Warfield's view are numerous, but perhaps the most extended recent treatment is that of Edward J. Young. According to him, "Inspiration is a superintendence of God the Holy Spirit over the writers of the Scriptures, as a result of which these Scriptures possess Divine authority and trustworthiness and, possessing such Divine authority and trustworthiness, are free from error."[24]

Tradition and Inerrancy

This historical survey reveals that there has been a traditional or classic doctrine of inspiration. With few exceptions the church has contended for both the human and the divine character of Scripture. For the greater part of this nineteen-hundred-year history, however, the existing manuscripts (both the Hebrew and Septuagint texts in the Old Testament and the Greek texts in the New Testament) were generally considered inspired.

But with the expansion of scientific knowledge Christians recognized increasingly the problems inherent in any attempt to reconcile the divine and human factors in the extant manuscripts of Scripture. In order to strengthen the essence of the traditional doctrine, more and more emphasis was placed on the original writings (autographs) as the basis of appeal for the inspiration, trustworthiness, and inerrancy of Scripture. We can agree heartily with the general affirmations of the traditional view of inspiration. The difficulties cluster around the *refinements* of the classic view that have come to the front since the beginning of the nineteenth century.

As A. G. Hebert comments, "Hence the inerrancy of the Bible, as it is understood today, is a new doctrine, and the modern fundamentalist is asserting something that no previous age has understood in anything like the modern sense." [25] Notwithstanding the clear historical evidence supporting this assertion, some evangelical scholars reject it with the utmost emphasis. The verbal, plenary view of inspiration "is the inspiration which the Scriptures claim for themselves, which the Apostolic Church claimed for them, and what the Reformed Church understood by the Word of God written." [26]

However, such a sweeping claim does not give sufficient weight to the following statement by Warfield and Hodge: "The word 'Inspiration,' as applied to the Holy Scriptures, has gradually acquired a specific technical meaning independent of its etymology. At first this word, in the sense of 'God-breathed,' was used to express the entire agency of God in producing that divine element which distinguishes Scripture from all other writings. It was used in a sense comprehensive of supernatural revelation, while the immense range of providential and gracious divine activities concerning the genesis of the word of God in human language was practically overlooked." [27] This statement is quite an accurate picture of the situation. The early definitions of inspiration were generalized and "in a sense comprehensive of supernatural revelation." It was only as systematic theology began to reckon with the data from science that the more technical, precise definitions of inspiration came into being. Some of the general statements of Scripture and church history concerning inspiration appear to be the same as the modern formulations of verbal plenary inspiration, but in most instances the *similarity is in appearance only* because the precise meaning of the words has changed in various ways. Only when Scripture and history of doctrine are read with the presupposition of inerrancy is it possible to extend the twentieth-century formulation of verbal-plenary, inerrant inspiration back through church history and even into Scripture itself.

8: *Revelation, Inspiration, and Existentialism*

As indicated in the previous chapters, the traditional view of inspiration has been conceived almost exclusively in terms of the book. The inspiration of the Biblical writers was never doubted, but the focus was on the written record—for many centuries the extant Scriptures and then later on the autographs. In the eighteenth and nineteenth centuries, however, some reactions set in against the pattern of church life and thought, the doctrine of Scripture included. While the liberal reaction was most prominent and influential during this period, there appeared a point of view that was in opposition both to liberalism and traditionalism.

Søren Kierkegaard and Existentialism

The spearhead of this new approach was Søren Kierkegaard (1813–1855) of Copenhagen, Denmark. He studied with the German philosopher Georg Hegel (1770–1831), but the pantheism and rationalism of his teacher only frustrated his quest for a warm, dynamic relationship with God. Abstract speculation or reason could never find God, Kierkegaard affirmed, because there is an "infinite qualitative difference" between time (man's realm) and eternity (God's realm). Finite mankind is incapable of knowing the divine, infinite, utterly transcendent God unless the latter breaks in upon him by spanning the gulf.

According to Kierkegaard, God, in taking the initiative, reveals himself through a continuous series of crises. At each "encounter" or "confrontation" man is faced with an *either-or:* either he yields his whole being to God or he bears the responsibility of rejecting God's claim on him. Knowledge comes at this moment of confrontation — it can never come through human reason. It is readily apparent why Kierkegaard rejected the cold ritualism and intellectual stress on doctrine that characterized the national Church in Denmark at this time. Its impersonal nature, he discerned, was due to the idea that God, Christ, and the Scriptures were *objects* to be examined, pondered over, and finally assented to. Christianity for Kierkegaard meant something within his being. Faith was a subjective leap made against anything human reason could furnish.

This contrast between objectivity and subjectivity was basic to all of Kierkegaard's thought. Because, according to him, no person could do both at the same time, the situation was an eternal *either-or.* His definition of essential truth (the truth that is essentially related to existence) is as follows: "When the question of truth is raised in an objective manner, reflection is directed objectively to the truth, as an object to which the knower is related. Reflection is not focused upon the relationship, however, but upon the question of whether it is the truth to which the knower is related. If only the object to which he is related is the truth, the subject is accounted to be in the truth. When the question of the truth is raised subjectively, reflection is directed subjectively to the nature of the individual's relationship; if only the mode of this relationship is in the truth, the individual is in the truth even if he should happen to be thus related to what is not true."[1] He expresses his theme in the summary statement, "*The objective accent falls on WHAT is said, the subjective accent on HOW it is said.*"[2]

In discussing the relative merits of the two approaches to truth, he writes: "Now when the problem is to reckon up on which side there is most truth, whether on the side of one who seeks the true God objectively, and pursues the approximate truth of the God-idea; or on the side of one who, driven by the infinite passion of his need of God, feels an infinite concern for his own relationship to God in truth (and to be at one and the same time on both sides equally, is as we have noted not possible for an existing individual, but is merely the happy delusion of an imaginary I-am-I): the answer cannot be in doubt for anyone who has not been demoralized with the aid of science. If one who lives in the midst of Christendom goes up to the house of God, the house of the true God, with the true conception of God in his knowledge, and prays, but prays in a false spirit; and one who lives in an idolatrous community prays with the entire passion of the infinite, although his eyes rest upon the image of an idol: where is there most truth? The one prays in truth to God though he worships an idol; the other prays falsely to the true God, and hence worships in fact an idol."[3] The references to "Christendom," "house of God," and praying "in a false spirit" are scars of the bitter disappointment he experienced in the church. A heathen praying passionately to an idol, "what is not true," is actually "in the truth." This is the extreme to which the stagnant Danish Church drove the warmhearted Kierkegaard. There is certainly some truth in this reaction, for "man looks on the outward appearance, but the Lord looks on the heart" (I Sam. 16:7). God will have more mercy on heathen with sincerity of heart than on hypocrites who frequent churches on Sunday for reasons of business or status.

However, Kierkegaard's views did not take hold in any great way during the nineteenth and early twentieth centuries. The liberalism of Schleiermacher, Ritschl, and Harnack, with its naïve optimism in the innate goodness and moral perfectibility of man, was too appealing. But when this fantasy was shattered by the shells of World War I, the mood began to change — the time was ripe for the insights of Søren Kierkegaard. While existentialism became the new frontier of thought, it took on many diverse interpretations: Russian Orthodox Nicholas Berdyaev (1874–1948); the Jew Martin Buber (1878–); German philosopher Martin Heidegger (1889–), whose non-Christian approach found full atheistic expression in his student, the Frenchman Jean-Paul Sartre (1905-); the German Lutheran Rudolf Bultmann (1884-), who, although indebted to Heidegger, remained within the Christian context; Swiss Reformed theologian Karl Barth (1886-); and his Swiss colleague Emil Brunner (1889-).

Barth and Brunner are the most orthodox of the existentialists, and until recently they had the greatest influence on the thinking of the church. Their interpretation of existentialism has been known as "neoorthodoxy" or "the new Reformation theology," because of its return to some traditional themes. The emphasis on crisis and decision gave rise to the designation "crisis theology." The method of expressing truths by a series of paradoxes or apparently contradictory statements evoked the title "dialectical theology."

New Reformation Theology and Revelation

It is necessary to begin with a brief consideration of "revelation," because, as James Orr contended, "the doctrine of inspiration grows out of that of revelation, and can only be made intelligible through the latter."[4] In the Old and New Testaments the concept of revelation is expressed in a number of ways, but the general meaning is "uncovering, opening to view, or disclosing what is hidden, unknown, or mysterious." For the greater part of the church's existence, "revelation" meant Scripture as a whole, and "inspiration" was used in a comprehensive sense referring to this supernatural or special unit of God's revelation to mankind. Thus, the two terms were almost synonymous in use and confined largely to Scripture.

It is now commonly acknowledged, however, that special revelation is broader than Scripture. Long before the *recording* of Old Testament events, revelation was a reality for those who were receptive to God's self-disclosure. Furthermore, some of God's revelatory deeds in behalf of his servants were never recorded and preserved for us. The New Testament is explicit at this point: "Now Jesus did many other signs in the presence of the disciples, which are not written in this book" (John 20:30). Scripture is that portion of redemptive history which was recorded and transmitted to us. It is implicit, however, that the record is sufficiently complete to lead to belief in Jesus Christ, the fullness of revelation, and thereby to eternal life.

Revelation and Response

Although the conservative tradition of the church acknowledges that revelation, in theory, is broader than Scripture, it contends, from a practical point of view, that Scripture *is* revelation because it is the only revelation extant. On the other hand, in line with its existential interpretation of Scripture, new Reformation theology defines "revelation" as something that can occur only between persons. According to Brunner: "In the New Testament faith is the relation between person and person, the obedient trust of man in the God who graciously stoops to meet him. Here revelation is 'truth as encounter,' and faith is knowledge as encounter." [5] Thus, "Revelation is something that *happens,* the living history of God in his dealings with the human race: the history of revelation is the history of salvation, and the history of salvation is the history of revelation. Both are the same, seen from two angles." [6] Accordingly, for Brunner and most of the contemporary theologians, Scripture, as a book, can never *be* revelation. At best it is an authentic record of, or witness to, God's redemptive acts in behalf of man. Revelation, in other words, is subjective. When one asserts that Scripture *is* revelation, one is making a value judgment on the basis of subjective reality derived through Scripture.

This point of view is illustrated by the account in John 20:24-29. Thomas, called the Twin, was not with the disciples when Jesus appeared to them, and so he refused to believe their story. Eight days later Jesus appeared to the disciples again and he specifically confronted Thomas with his nail-scarred hands and his wounded side. This encounter was revelation to Thomas and he exclaimed, "My Lord and my God!" Jesus is then reported to have said: " Have you believed because you have seen me? Blessed are those who have not seen and yet believe." The precise act of Jesus' appearing to Thomas cannot be revelation for us — we were not there. But the record of Jesus' disclosure to Thomas becomes the *means of revelation* to us. Even though we cannot see as Thomas saw, nevertheless, if we take the account seriously, the Holy Spirit confronts us with his witness. In that moment of encounter and faith, revelation becomes a reality for us and we exclaim with Thomas, " My Lord and my God! "

Those who hold that Scripture *is* revelation acknowledge that if revelation is to be an accomplished fact and to have practical significance, Scripture must have the response of the hearer or reader. It is beyond question, therefore, that revelation must be defined subjectively if the term is to be in accord with the facts. Where tradition really differs from the new Reformation theology is in its interpretation of the content and objective nature of Scripture, especially the matter of doctrine. But these issues, which will be considered later, do not negate the basic truth inherent in this new understanding of revelation.

New Reformation Theology and Inspiration

Whereas revelation has to do with the substance and meaning of God's self-disclosure, inspiration is concerned with the giving and receiving of the redemptive message. Accordingly, the definition of inspiration in the new Reformation theology is also primarily in terms of events wherein the Holy Spirit illumines Scripture for those who hear and read. This emphasis is not to deny the original acts of inspiration, for as Barth declares: " We cannot speak of the inspiration of the Bible without that royal act of the original inspiration in which the risen Christ gave his own a part in his own divine Spirit. But no more can we speak of it without that other royal act — which is only a continuation of the first — in which the inspiration is imparted to us, in which here and now we are forced out of our position as spectators of the word and work of the Biblical writers, in which the calling of the prophets and apostles becomes an event to us by the ministry of their word and work." [7]

The Bible, therefore, is the means by which the Holy Spirit completes the circle of inspiration that he began with the Biblical writers. To what extent can one speak of the inspiration of the Biblical text? Barth rejects "verbal inspiration" in the traditional sense. This concept he calls "verbal inspiredness." According to him: "Verbal inspiration does not mean the infallibility of the Biblical word in its linguistic, historical, and theological character as a human word. It means that the fallible and faulty human word is as such used by God and has to be received and heard in spite of its human fallibility." [8] The Bible *is* the Word of God because "God himself now says what the text says. The work of God is done through this text. The miracle of God takes place in this text formed of human words." [9]

Concerning this event which turns spectators into participants, Barth comments: "If, therefore, we are serious about the fact that this miracle is an event, we cannot regard the presence of God's Word in the Bible as an attribute inhering once for all in this book as such and what we see before us of books and chapters and verses. Of the book as we have it, we can only say: We recollect that we have heard in this book the Word of God; we recollect, in and with the church, that the Word of God has been heard in all this book and in all parts of it; therefore we expect that we shall hear the Word of God in this book again, and hear it even in those places where we ourselves have not heard it before. Yet the presence of the Word of God itself, the real and present speaking and hearing of it, is not identical with the existence of the book as such. But in this presence something takes place in and with the book, for which the book as such does indeed give the possibility, but the reality of which cannot be anticipated or replaced by the existence of the book. A free divine decision is made. It then comes about that the Bible, the Bible *in concreto,* this or that Biblical context, i.e., the Bible as it comes to us in this or that specific measure, is taken and used as an instrument in the hand of God, i.e., it speaks to and is heard by us as the authentic witness to divine revelation and is therefore present as the Word of God. It is present in a way we cannot conceive: not as a third time between past and future, between recollection and expectation, but as that point between the two which we cannot think of as time, which when it is considered immediately becomes once more either before or after." [10]

Thus the Bible, the written Word, becomes God's Word when the Word of God, the risen Christ, speaks through the message of the prophets and apostles. Inspiration, therefore, is being caught up into God's time. The moment this experience is considered, it ceases — its subjective, existential character is transmuted into an object, something over which to ponder. In returning to the chronological time of man's world, all that one can do is recall the past moment of inspiration or anticipate another encounter. But the miraculous event does not lie with man. While he can read Scripture with expectancy, he cannot coerce a confrontation with the Word of God. Inspiration is God's free, divine act, and as such, man must knock and wait. "The door of the Bible texts," Barth declares, "can be opened only from within." [11]

But this opening of the text is the work of God's Spirit, not the Biblical text itself. Accordingly, one is not warranted in assigning inspiration to the book; one can read the Bible and still not be confronted with the Word of God. Stress on the book was, in Barth's opinion, the error of the seventeenth-century theologians. In this view "the Word of God could no longer be the Word of God and therefore it was no longer recognized as such. The Bible was now grounded upon itself apart from the mystery of Christ and the Holy Ghost. It became a 'paper pope,' and unlike the living pope in Rome it was wholly given up into the hands of its interpreters. It was no longer a free and spiritual force, but an instrument of human power." [12] Barth opposes the supranaturalism of inerrancy because it is not radical enough. With respect to the writings of the prophets and apostles he affirms: "To the bold postulate, that if their word is to be the Word of God they must be inerrant in every word, we oppose the even bolder assertion, that according to the Scriptural witness about man, which applies to them too, they can be at fault in any word, and have been at fault in every word, and yet according to the same Scriptural witness, being justified and sanctified by grace alone, they have still spoken the Word of God in their fallible and erring human word." [13] Whereas the supranaturalism of inerrancy is focused on the recording of revelation in the autographs, the supranaturalism of Barth's view is centered in that existential miracle by which the human word of the Bible comes alive as the Word of God.

Barth's view of inspiration is epitomized in the following summary: " We can sum up all that must be said on this point in the statement that faith in the inspiration of the Bible stands or falls by whether the concrete life of the church and of the members of the church is a life really dominated by the exegesis of the Bible. If the Biblical text in its literalness as a text does not force itself upon us, or if we have the freedom word by word to shake ourselves loose from it, what meaning is there in our protestation that the Bible is inspired and the Word of God? To say 'Lord, Lord' is not enough. What matters is to do the will of God if we are to know His grace and truth — for that is the inspiration of the Bible." [14] Inspiration, like revelation, is defined with primary emphasis on the subjective, existential aspects of reality.

On the other hand, although Barth shies away from any statement that would attribute inspiration to the written record, the doctrine of inerrancy has not been more forthright in declaring the absolute *indispensability of Scripture*. In discussing the relative authority of Scripture and the church, Barth affirms: " Consequently the church cannot evade Scripture. It cannot try to appeal past it directly to God, to Christ, or to the Holy Spirit. It cannot assess and adjudge Scripture from a view of revelation gained apart from Scripture and not related to it. It cannot know any 'normal dignity,' which has to sanctify Scripture as the earliest record of its own life and make it its norm. It cannot establish from any possession of revelation the fact and extent that

Scripture too is a source of revelation. Scripture confronts it commandingly as Holy Scripture, and it receives revelation from it in an encounter which is just as concrete and concretely ordered as that which according to Scripture originally took place between the Lord and his witnesses. It obeys Holy Scripture. Not as though it were obeying some long-deceased men and their humanity and theology. But it obeys the One whom it has pleased to give certain long-deceased men, in and with and in spite of their humanity and piety and theology, a commission and authority. Therefore it serves the Word of God in the sign and guise of the word of these men. As it hears *them,* it hears it. And as it hears them, it *hears* it. The incarnation of the Word of God and the outpouring of the Holy Spirit has happened, is happening, and will happen for the church (and through the church for the world) in every age, because in face of the uniqueness of revelation the church is ready to receive its authentic witness and to accept and transmit it as authentic." [15] Scripture, as a product of inspiration, has certain characteristics that set it apart from other literature; thus it is the necessary *means of inspiration*. In theory, therefore, Barth (who denies the reality of general revelation) claims there can be no response and revelation if there is no hearing or reading of Scripture. Even for Brunner, who accepts the fact of general revelation, there can be no special revelation without response to Scripture.

While Barth and Brunner do not discount the Bible as the objective record of redemptive history, they hesitate to define the book in terms of revelation and inspiration. Once this is done, so they claim, the words of Scripture tend to take on an authoritarian role that results in mere assent by the hearer or reader rather than in a genuine experience of faith and response. It is a fact of church history that undue stress on the Book has often resulted in a religion of assent which stopped short of genuine faith in Jesus Christ. Notwithstanding this extreme, however, many who have defined inspiration and revelation *solely* in terms of Scripture have come to a vital faith in Christ. In such cases the Bible did not become a "paper pope." Conversely, an existential definition of revelation and inspiration is no guarantee that the person who holds it will encounter Christ through Scripture. Humble submission to the Christ back of Scripture is far more crucial than one's doctrine of revelation and inspiration. Doctrine is not to be discounted, but the ultimate in fellowship with God is *being* " in Christ."

Revelation and Communication

The debate over Scripture's role in redemption is somewhat similar to the old argument as to whether there would be a sound if a tree fell in the woods and there was no animal or human being to hear it. We know now that hearing takes place in the mind. The ear is simply an organ for converting air waves into electrical impulses. In reality, therefore, sound is dependent on the organs of receptivity and response. This concession, however, does not eliminate the necessity of the falling tree and the resultant air waves. Without these the ear and mind would wait in vain—there would be no sound.

Putting the matter simply, revelation (like communication) has three essential factors: (1) a communicator or source, (2) his message, and (3) the response of the receiver. If any one of the three is missing, there is no revelation or communication. In making his self-disclosure, God, the communicator, employed various means. Of primary importance were his great redemptive acts in behalf of Abraham, Isaac, Jacob, Moses, and the Children of Israel. Also in " many and various ways God spoke of old . . . by the prophets " (Heb. 1:1). Finally God sent his Son as the fullness of revelation. In each of God's acts, revelation became a reality for those who responded favorably. Reports of these moments of encounter with God were passed on orally at first, and then in due time they were reduced to writing. In any case, most of the Israelites and the Jews were dependent on reports or records of revelation, and, aside from the earliest Christians, the same has been true of the church. The vast majority of God's creatures have not been favored with such extraordinary self-disclosures as depicted in Scripture. Evidently the record of redemptive history is sufficient, when enlightened by the Holy Spirit, to achieve God's purpose.

Inasmuch as inspiration grows out of revelation, a comprehensive doctrine of inspiration will also include three aspects. First of all, there was the influence of God's Spirit in each of the exceedingly varied ways by which God made himself known. This same Spirit was at work in the task of recording for posterity some of the deeds and words associated with God's redemptive activity. Then by means of the record, whether the autograph or a copy, the Spirit of God spoke to the hearer or reader. Thus, the history of Israel and the church has been characterized by countless situations in which Scripture, the product of inspiration, has become the means of revelation and inspiration. Of the many more-or-less traditional definitions of inspiration, perhaps the best example of this three-faceted view is the definition given by Augustus H. Strong: "Inspiration is that influence of the Spirit of God upon the minds of the Scripture writers which made their writings the record of a progressive divine revelation, sufficient, when taken together and interpreted by the same Spirit who inspired them, to lead every honest inquirer to Christ and to salvation."[16] Whereas traditionalism in general has stressed the role of the Book, the new Reformation theology has reminded the church that if revelation and inspiration are to be complete, they must be actualized in the lives of persons.

9: *Revelation, Inspiration, and Doctrine*

WHILE the new Reformation theology is technically accurate in defining revelation and inspiration in terms of personal communication between God and man, this fact does not eliminate the need for detailed discussion of Scripture, the indispensable means of revelation. If one grants, for the moment, the traditional definition of revelation and inspiration, there is the issue of how these two doctrinal formulations are related to each other and to the Bible. Furthermore, consideration must be given to the basic matter of ascertaining the significance and role of teaching, doctrine, or propositional truth in the record of revelation. One's use and interpretation of Scripture is, after all, a very crucial factor in the practical outworkings of one's doctrine of revelation and inspiration.

Revelation and Inspiration

As noted previously, for the greater part of the church's existence the two terms "inspiration" and "revelation" were considered almost synonymous. Warfield and Hodge were correct in declaring: "The word 'Inspiration,' as applied to the Holy Scriptures, has gradually acquired a specific technical meaning independent of its etymology. At first this word . . . was used in a sense comprehensive of supernatural revelation."[1] In defense of this technical refinement they contended: "It is important that distinguishable ideas should be connoted by distinct terms, and that the terms themselves should be fixed in a definite sense. Thus we have come to distinguish sharply between Revelation, which is the frequent, and Inspiration, which is the constant, attribute of all thoughts and statements of Scripture." [2]

The assertion that revelation is the variable element in Scripture while inspiration is the constant factor, applying equally well to every word of the canon, is a theologian's deduction. Obviously the two ideas are not precisely the same, but the teachings and the data of Scripture do not warrant the "fixed" meanings assigned by Hodge and Warfield. In general the Scriptures associate inspiration with God's acts of self-disclosure to his servants.

Concerning the relation of inspiration to the record of revelation, Orr comments: "It is urged . . . that unless we can demonstrate what is called the 'inerrancy' of the Biblical record, down even to its minutest details, the whole edifice of belief in revealed religion falls to the ground. This, on the face of it, is a most suicidal position for any defender of revelation to take up. It is certainly a much easier matter to prove the reality of a divine revelation in the history of Israel, or in Christ, than it is to prove the inerrant inspiration of every part of the record, through which that revelation has come to us. Grant the Gospels to be only ordinary historical documents — trustworthy records of the life of Christ, apart from any special inspiration in their authors — we should still, one may contend, be shut up as much as ever to the belief that the Person whose words and works they narrate was One who made superhuman claims, and whose character, words, and deeds attested the truth of these claims." [3]

We know that Luke, the physician, was a companion of Paul on some of his journeys. Being a man of science, he used his trained mind to search out the available sources, and in checking the data he undoubtedly talked to all the eyewitnesses of Jesus he could find. Yet concerning his researches for writing Luke-Acts he says simply, "It seemed good to me also . . . to write." In what precise way was the inspiration of Luke different from that of any man of God today? There are hundreds of well-trained, devoted, meticulous Christians filled with God's Spirit today who could do as accurate a piece of reporting as Luke did. When Luke felt the urge to write " an orderly account " was his inspiration of a *different kind* from that of the Holy Spirit's activity in the hearts and minds of God's servants down through the history of the church? Not likely.

What distinguishes Luke from Christians today is not inspiration as such, but rather the unique period of revelation which he was privileged to witness. The same can be said for Mark, who learned from the lips of Peter the events of Christ's ministry on earth.

On the other hand, Luke refers to many other writers who undertook to compile a Gospel narrative. They wrote prior to Luke, and the implication is that they too had some relationship to this unique period of history. Then why were their accounts rejected while Luke's became a part of the canon? Apparently Luke himself gives us the answer. He had " followed all things closely [accurately] for some time past," and as a result he wrote " an orderly account." The clear implication is that the other accounts were not as orderly or accurate. But Luke's accuracy, while superior to the others he mentions, hardly comes under the category of unique inspiration. Therefore, it is (1) his association with Paul, the uniquely inspired servant of God, and (2) his own experience in that crucial period of history, which constitute Luke's uniqueness as a Biblical writer.

Degrees of Inspiration?

The Jews took a view of the Hebrew canon that amounted to degrees of inspiration. The Torah was supreme — no prophet was inspired as Moses was. Philo accepted this view and evidenced it in practice by confining almost all of his activity to the Pentateuch.

In reaction to the concept of " constant inspiration," as advocated during the nineteenth century, the idea of " degrees of inspiration " was renewed and expanded. William Sanday espoused this view in his Bampton Lectures of 1893. He explains briefly: "In other words, there are some books in which the Divine element is at the *maximum* and others in which it is at the *minimum*. When we come to reflect, it may be seen that the lower modes have a place in relation to the Divine purpose (which includes both high and low) that is not less appropriate than the higher, but from our present standpoint they must be described as lower."[4] Hebert, objecting to this doctrine, expresses himself as follows: "The distinction thus made between Revelation and Inspiration justifies itself by the close connection made by 'conservative' writers between Inspiration and Canonicity. It is true that this connection was made to justify the Inerrancy of the Bible at all points, and we have said that this is to be discounted; yet it was substantially sound, because it was an assertion that the Bible as a whole is inspired; and this, as we have seen, is necessary when the Bible is viewed as the Book of the divine Kingdom. When the Bible is so viewed, it becomes possible to assert both that the Bible as a whole is inspired, as being the record of the Sacred History which is consummated in Christ, and at the same time freely to recognize the imperfection of the human recipients of the revelation."[5]

Clearly, Hebert does not accept the doctrine of inerrancy. He is concerned, however (as all Christians should be), to claim the distinctiveness of the canonical Scriptures, and therefore he contends for a consistent level of inspiration. In spite of the imperfections of Scripture, the canon as a whole can be described legitimately as inspired by God. In this general sense, therefore, all the books are equally inspired. Although tied to canonicity, this definition of inspiration, let it be noted, is far removed from the definition that considers this constant factor of inspiration as the *guarantee of inerrancy* for every word.

The phenomena and statements of Scripture concerning its inspiration are so extensive and complex it is difficult to reckon adequately with all the data without deriving a formulation with varieties of inspiration. With respect to the intuition, illumination, dictation, and dynamic views of inspiration, Olin A. Curtis states: "There is, I am convinced, no worthy reason for holding one of these theories to the exclusion of the remaining three. The probability is that the Word of God was given by a combination of all four methods; but it is not now possible for us to decide in every case precisely what took place. The data are not sufficient." [6]

Curtis ties in this more comprehensive view of inspiration with the long historic process of God's redemptive activity. In this process "men were chosen, each one in his own peculiar situation, to speak, or to write, or to do, whatever was essential to further the redemptional movement." [7] Then he elaborates: "For this furtherance, these chosen men received only such divine help as was needed. At one time it was necessary only to emphasize a common moral fact before the people, and any brave soul could do it. At another time it was necessary to lift a commonplace into spiritual ideality, a work which only genius can do. At another time it was necessary to organize a nation, and it required the highest order of statesmanship. At another time it was necessary to have a Christian testimony, and it could be given out of any overflowing Christian experience in the early church. At another time it was necessary to catch and to express a doctrine of grace entirely beyond the possibility of natural discovery; and for this work a man was extraordinarily helped, raised to a higher power, without being erased as a free person. At another time it was necessary for the man of God to have an absolutely transcendent experience, an experience to which he could make no individual or personal contribution whatever; and he was, for the occasion, actually coerced by the Holy Spirit. He had no more freedom than the sky has in accepting a sunset. Perhaps he is a prophet, and he looks down the centuries, in the swift, clear vision of God himself, until he can see 'a man of sorrows'—'smitten of God,' 'wounded for our transgressions.' Or perhaps he is an apostle, and he is transported into a realm of immeasurable glory, and hears 'unspeakable words, which it is not lawful for a man to utter.' There are, too, some places in the Bible where the best explanation of the very phrase is that it came directly from God. And when I say the best explanation, I mean the explanation which naturally grows out of the Christian conception of God's relation to man in redemption. How extremely absurd it is for any Christian thinker to hold that God could not or would not, in the furtherance of redemption, give a prophet or an apostle a message as definite as human speech. Even the most incipient Christian theist should be ashamed of such fundamental inconsistency." [8]

All these activities of God's servants derived from inspiration of some sort, and so with Hebert we can speak of the Bible as being inspired from cover to cover, human mistakes and all. On the other hand, all of Scripture does not involve special revelation, and so there is no need to posit *unique* inspiration for every word of the Bible. There are degrees of something in Scripture, and it is more than just degrees of revelation. As Orr observes, "It does not follow that all inspired persons possess the Spirit in a *like* eminent degree. Inspiration in Scripture is of different kinds, and for different ends. It is certainly too narrow an idea of inspiration to tie it down to the production of the written record. There is inspiration in speech as well as in writing; and there are lower grades of inspiration in the form of special *charismata* (wisdom, artistic skill, physical powers), shading off till it becomes difficult to distinguish them from heightened natural endowment." [9] He explains further as follows: "But the fact is obvious that, whereas at some periods and in some souls the Spirit of revelation is working, if one may so say, at a maximum, at other times, and in other persons, He is operating on a lower plane, and, still to speak reverently, with feebler energy. Every one, by a species of 'higher criticism' of his own, recognizes this in practice, whatever he may do in theory. No one . . . would compare the Books of Chronicles, in point of spirituality, with the prophecies of Isaiah or the Gospel of John, or the books of Esther and Ecclesiastes, as to the canonicity of which the later Jews themselves had doubts, with the Epistles of Paul. The prophets after the exile stand, on the whole, on a lower plane than the earlier prophets — Hosea, Amos, Isaiah, etc. In the natural body, as Paul reminds us, all members have not the same office, and so is it here. Some parts of Scripture have a humbler function to fulfill than others." [10]

If it is true that God's activities with his servants involved varying degrees of " inspiration " and " divine help," how is one justified in speaking of the written record of these events as equally inspired? The idea that inspiration is the constant factor throughout Scripture, applying equally to every book and word, is a theological deduction, not an explicit teaching of the Bible. The line of deductive reasoning commences with the assumption that God had to reveal himself infallibly. To guarantee this absolute accuracy, God's Spirit superintended all the activity of the chosen instruments to the end that every word of their written records was inerrant and thus equally inspired. As a corollary of this view only those books included in the standard Protestant canon were superintended (that is, inspired) by God.

But any definition of inspiration that places primary importance on the autographs of the canonical books is far from the well-rounded idea of inspiration set forth in Scripture. The canon *as a whole* will always rank as uniquely inspired literature because it is God's chosen means of revealing himself to us. As noted previously, however, the fringes of this unique collection are tattered in places, yet without marring the essence of the whole. This principle was recognized by the translators of the King James Version in their preface: " For it is confessed, that things are to take their denomination of the greater part. . . . A man may be counted a virtuous man, though he have made many slips in his life, (else there were none virtuous, for, in many things we offend all) also a comely man and lovely, though he have some warts upon his hand, yea, not only freckles upon his face, but also scars." Because this is also true in the realm of Scripture, we are not justified in claiming that every word in the Biblical canon is the product of unique inspiration any more than we are warranted in denying that some portions of noncanonical writings came into being through the working of God's Spirit in the hearts of men.

Inspiration — Ancient and Modern

The practical priority that revelation has over inspiration can be illustrated by imagining that all religious literature has been destroyed except the canonical book Song of Songs and the beautiful hymn of Isaac Watts, "When I Survey the Wondrous Cross." Given only one choice, which of the two would one choose? According to traditional definitions, the Biblical book is inspired in a special sense whereas the hymn is not, but it is doubtful that most Christians would choose Song of Songs. Although Watts wrote long after the close of the canon, his hymn is grounded in the revelation of Christ's vicarious death and has far greater value in and of itself than does the Old Testament love song.

Some of the psalms are simply an exhortation to praise God because of his dealings with Israel. The psalmist repeats well-known facts and out of the fullness of his experience with God exhorts his brethren to greater lives of devotion to Israel's loving God. Some of the great hymns are practically on a par with the psalms, and one can be sure that if Isaac Watts, Charles Wesley, Augustus Toplady, and Reginald Heber had lived in the time of David and Solomon and been *no more inspired than they were in their own day,* some of their hymns of praise to God would have found their way into the Hebrew canon.

Some hymn writers, in fact, have had experiences bordering on those of the Biblical writers. The Scottish minister George Matheson, for example, wrote the lovely hymn "O Love That Will Not Let Me Go" during a time of personal distress. It was on the evening of June 6, 1882, while the whole family went to his sister's wedding in Glasgow, that something happened to him which caused "the most severe mental suffering." Alone in the manse of Inellan, apparently the thoughts of his sister's marriage brought to mind the traumatic experience of his youth, more than twenty years before, when his fiancée, notwithstanding his consuming love for her, rejected him because he was going blind. Concerning this period of mental depression, Matheson writes,

"The hymn was the fruit of that suffering. It was the quickest bit of work I ever did in my life. I had the impression rather of having it dictated to me by some inward voice than of working it out myself. I am quite sure that the whole work was completed in five minutes, and equally sure that it never received at my hands any retouching or correction. I have no natural gift of rhythm. All the other verses I have written are manufactured articles; this came like a dayspring from on high. I have never been able to gain once more the same fervor in verse." [11]

Undoubtedly, God's Spirit spoke in this vital way to the troubled soul of George Matheson. This is the kind of inspiration of which the psalms were made. There is no difference in kind. If there is any difference, it is a matter of degree. When the Biblical writers served as channels of God's revelation they needed more divine help, but the inspiration was not distinct in kind from that given to all the messengers of God down through history. What distinguishes the Bible is its record of special revelation, not a distinctive kind of inspiration.

If the church had a more dynamic sense of God's inspiration in the twentieth century, it would be more effective in its witness and outreach. It is well and good to protect the distinctiveness of the Bible, but to think only in terms of its inspiration as absolutely different in kind from inspiration in our time is too high a price to pay. Christians today need to have the same sense of being God-motivated and God-sent as did the Biblical writers. In a sense, the difficulty of interpreting God's record of revelation to this complex age requires almost as much of God's inbreathing and wisdom as did the original experiences of revelation.

Orthodoxy and Doctrine

"Orthodoxy," a term derived from the Greek word *orthodoxos* (*orthos,* "straight, upright" + *doxa,* "opinion, thinking"), has been used to designate that portion of the church which has defined revelation primarily in terms of teaching or doctrine. Orthodoxy has not been ignorant of God's historical acts, but correct doctrine has been considered to be the ultimate criterion of a Christian.

This emphasis on teaching has some basis in the Old Testament, especially with respect to the law. Moses is commanded to teach Israel commandments, statutes, and ordinances (Ex. 24:12; Deut. 6:1) and this teaching ministry is in turn assigned to the priests (Lev. 10:11; Deut. 33:10). The primary purpose of this teaching is obedience and correct practice (orthopraxy) rather than correct doctrine (orthodoxy).

The clearest exhortations in behalf of correct doctrine come from the later books of the New Testament: "All scripture is inspired by God and profitable for teaching" (II Tim. 3:16); "For the time is coming when people will not endure sound teaching" (II Tim. 4:3); "Therefore rebuke them sharply, that they may be sound in the faith" (Titus 1:13); "But as for you, teach what befits sound doctrine" (Titus 2:1); "So that in everything they may adorn the doctrine of God our Savior" (Titus 2:10); "To contend for the faith which was once for all delivered to the saints" (Jude 3).

It is quite evident why this stress on doctrine, a package of truth called "the faith," became so prominent as the church expanded. While the Lord was still with the disciples, the outstanding feature was the vitality of his fellowship with them. This was also true of Saul in those first years after he yielded himself to the Lord on the way to Damascus. Later on, however, the apostles, with opposition on all sides, felt compelled to give greater attention to matters of content and doctrine. Many different ideas were afloat, both inside and outside the early church, and there were men with missionary zeal to promote them. Since Christ was gone, the next most authoritative source was the apostles, and in meeting the challenge of these new ideas they appealed to their experiences of fellowship and instruction with Jesus. As time widened the gap between the ascension and the expanding church the essential core of teaching crystallized into "the faith." The early church fathers considered it their primary task to carry on the struggle against heresies, and so their writings consist largely of *apologia,* "defense" of the gospel.

Following the Reformation in 1517 and the accompanying spiritual awakening, the young Protestant Church, not unlike the early church, found itself confronted with antagonists on all sides — the Roman Catholic Church as well as the secular world of science and philosophy. In its desperate fight for existence, doctrine became the chief weapon. During the seventeenth century — a century filled with wars and characterized by hatred and unbridled attacks against any and all opponents — the Protestant theologians often fought viciously, trying to maintain the truth of God. What they failed to see was that *love,* the greatest and most powerful force in God's Kingdom, was itself a part of doctrine, and that no defense of doctrine, however sincere, could really please God unless it was done in love.

The Reaction to Doctrine

It seems to be a law of nature that extremes beget extremes, and so undue emphasis on doctrine has brought forth a decided reaction which tends to repudiate all doctrine. According to this view, the early emphasis in the New Testament was "believe in," an expression of dynamic personal faith. This was also true of Paul, with his favorite expression "in Christ." Later on, the emphasis was "believe that," for example, Heb. 11:6, "For whoever would draw near to God must believe that he exists and that he rewards those who seek him." To "believe that," so it is affirmed, was spiritual degradation from the early fellowship, which said "believe in."

The classic expression of this viewpoint was made by Archbishop William Temple in his Gifford Lectures, *Nature, Man and God.* "The primary fact concerning revelation in its essence," writes Temple, "is that it is a personal self-disclosure to persons, and has authority as such." [12] The late Scottish theologian John Baillie explains further: "All revelation, then, is from subject to subject, and the revelation with which we are here concerned is from the divine Subject to the human. But there is a further distinction that must be drawn. We speak, as has been said, of a man's revealing himself, that is, his character and mind and will, to his fellow, but we also sometimes speak of a man's revealing to his fellow certain items of knowledge other than knowledge of himself. . . . According to the Bible, what is revealed to us is not a body of information concerning various things of which we might otherwise be ignorant. If it is information at all, it is information concerning the nature and mind and purpose of God—that and nothing else. Yet in the last resort it is not information about God that is revealed, but very God himself incarnate in Jesus Christ our Lord."[13]

In a similar vein, C. H. Dodd, the Cambridge University scholar, writes: "Jesus was primarily concerned not with delivering 'doctrine,' but with making men anew, so that they could receive the revelation of himself which God is always seeking to communicate. Similarly, the most important thing we find in the Bible is not 'doctrine' but something that helps us into a new attitude to God and to life."[14] Brunner expresses this point of view as follows: "In the time of the apostles, as in that of the Old Testament prophets, 'divine revelation' always meant the whole of the divine activity for the salvation of the world, the whole story of God's saving acts, of the 'acts of God' which reveal God's nature and his will, above all, him in whom the preceding revelation gains its meaning, and who therefore is its fulfillment: Jesus Christ. He himself is the Revelation. Divine revelation is not a book or a doctrine; the Revelation is God himself in his self-manifestation within history."[15] Baillie was certainly correct when he observed that this concept of revelation "is the first thing we notice as running broadly throughout all the recent discussions, marking them off from the formulations of earlier periods."[16]

Two Kinds of Truth

Basic to an understanding of this qualitative distinction between revelation and doctrine is the recognition that there are two different kinds of truth: objective and subjective. Objective truth is rational truth which has to do with "things" or "objects" — not only *concrete* things found in the material world all about us but also *abstract* things in the realm of ideas, values, laws, and culture. Since it is ascertained by means of reason, and thus impersonal in nature, objective truth is referred to as "it-truth."

Subjective truth, on the other hand, is personal because it involves the heart and happens only between persons. The difference between the two kinds of truth is quite evident even on the level of human love. One can read love stories and understand the psychology of love, but this rational knowledge or "it-truth" can never be the "thou-truth" which two people in love experience.

The qualitative gap between objective and subjective truth is much clearer, however, when it comes to the realm of man's spiritual needs. Here the "thou" of true love between husband and wife, or the "thou" of true brotherly love, is ineffectual. As Brunner observes, "the 'thou' of my fellow man cannot give me what I need, because he is only my — equally poor — fellow self. He cannot give me the truth which is life, because he possesses only the truth that I also possess."[17]

A rational knowledge about God is not the answer either, because it is not the true "Thou" which makes me a new creature in Christ. With respect to thoughts about God, Brunner comments: "Even God is here part of *my* rational world, in which I am the center; even he is the *Object* of my knowledge. It is true that I think of him as Subject, as the absolute Subject; but I myself am the subject of this thought; it is *my* thought; I introduce God into the world of my thought. Nothing happens that breaks through the circle of my self-isolation. I am alone with my truth, even with my idea of God. The God whom I think, is not the one who really confronts me."[18] He explains this "it-truth" more fully as follows: "All the transcendence that I think out for myself is only transcendence within immanence; all that I describe as *thou* within this my world of immanence is only 'thou-within-the-world-of-the-self.' This world of immanence, in spite of all the variety that takes place within it, is at bottom a static system. No real communication takes place. God does not communicate himself because I simply think *about* God, and that is all."[19]

One should not imply, however, that "it-truth" is untrue. God as creator is responsible for all truth. There is objective truth because God is also concerned with the impersonal realm of things and objects, but to appropriate rational truth is not to experience newness of life. The distinctiveness of "Thou-truth" is clearly set forth by Brunner: "This truth cannot therefore be appropriated in one act of objective perception of truth, but only in an *act of personal surrender and decision*. In order to gain this truth, not only must we make room for it, but we must 'die' in order that we may be raised by Christ to a new way of life. We cannot 'possess' this truth as we can 'possess other truths,' but we must *be* in this truth, we must *live* this truth, we must *do* it."[20]

Revelation and Doctrine

Undoubtedly the uniqueness of the Christian life is the experience of being "in Christ." But if we are to continue in the truth and doing the truth, there must be repeated encounters in which God reveals more of his will to us by the aid of the Holy Spirit. The means for maintaining this dynamic experience with God is the Bible. As a record of redemptive history—both the events and the interpretation of the events—Scripture is "it-truth." Without the Bible there would be no special revelation and without doctrine there would be no true faith. In approaching man, God must begin at the point of contact, namely, man's ability to reason. Accordingly, a minimal amount of theological ideas or teaching is necessary as a prerequisite for true faith. Sound doctrine is also necessary during the maturing of Christian experience, both for the individual and for the church.

Notwithstanding the indispensability of correct doctrine, there is no assurance that this rational, objective truth will lead to or preserve genuine faith. On this point, Brunner declares: " Christian doctrine, it is true, springs from the Word of God; but the Word of God is different from Christian doctrine. Faith cannot exist apart from sound doctrine, it is true, but it is not itself the understanding of doctrines. It is possible to hold correct views of doctrine without faith — and, indeed, in the course of the history of the church very many people have held correct doctrinal views without possessing genuine faith. Correct doctrine is something that can be learned, and indeed anyone who has a good brain and is able to study at a good college or university can learn it easily. But faith is not something that a man can 'learn'; it is the free gift of God. It is extremely bad for the church to confuse that which is the gift of the Holy Spirit alone with that which anyone with a good brain can learn at a good college." [21]

The futility of employing orthodox doctrine as the ultimate criterion for evaluating Christian experience is made explicit in the following statement from Brunner: " We would now add further that it is possible to understand the new message of the apostle Paul completely, intellectually and logically, and that means theologically, without having real faith. The believer, it is true, will reply, 'Then the message has not been rightly understood!' But the difference between an understanding based on genuine faith and the kind that can coexist with unbelief cannot be proved in intellectual terms. An unbeliever can pass the stiffest theological examination and prove that he understands 'Pauline theology' so well that no examiner could find any fault with his answers — and yet in the sense of spiritual understanding based on real faith he has understood nothing, but has remained a complete pagan. The Devil would pass the most rigorous examination in dogmatic and Biblical theology with distinction. Theology stands very close to the Word of God, but it is not itself the Word. Sound doctrine springs from the Word of God and from faith, but it is possible to understand it intellectually, to reproduce it theologically, and to make it part of one's intellectual equipment apart from faith. Faith, it is true, must pass through an understanding of theological ideas, even if they are very simple ones, but is not itself theological understanding."[22]

This insight has frightening implications for all those who handle the " sacred things " of Scripture. Regardless of one's location in the theological spectrum, there is the ever-present danger of knowing the truth objectively, but not being in it subjectively. It is imperative, therefore, that revelation and doctrine be distinguished. "Here, and here alone," says Brunner, " lies the gulf between this world and the world beyond, between reason and revelation. That is why a person who has long ago given up faith can still go on for a long time teaching correct theology. It is always at his disposal. But there is one thing that he can no longer do: he can no longer pray from his heart."[23]

Revelation and Propositional Truth

Just as traditional, conservative Christianity has endeavored to protect Scripture by equating revelation and doctrine, so it has contended that revelation is a series of eternal, timeless truths set in propositional form. Conversely, most of the recent theologians have affirmed that revelation is not a set of eternal truths. Here again, however, the points of view are not nearly so divergent as they would appear. The problem is really one of semantics—either the failure or unwillingness to understand one another. Contemporary theologies do not deny that there are timeless truths in the realm of objective truth. Their basic assertion is that eternal or propositional truths, like doctrine, cannot be considered as revelation because they cannot save. Even before existentialism took hold, P. T. Forsyth declared, "There are doctrines of salvation but no saving doctrines."[24]

Nevertheless, the Holy Spirit does not engender true faith apart from Scripture, a written record replete with teaching and objective truths. Nothwithstanding the differences between John and the three other Gospels, all four depict the life of Christ primarily in terms of teaching (by parables and discourses) which is authenticated by miracles or signs. The concern with content is clearly stated in Mark 4:33-34: " With many such parables he spoke the word to them, as they were able to hear it; he did not speak to them without a parable, but privately to his own disciples he explained everything." In the Gospels one of the most common titles for Jesus is "teacher." When many of Jesus' larger group of disciples murmured at his comments about the bread of life, he declared to them, " The words that I have spoken to you are spirit and life " (John 6:63). After many of the disciples drew back and Jesus asked the Twelve whether they too would go away, Peter affirmed, " You have the words of eternal life " (John 6:68). In another discourse Jesus said to the Jews, " If you continue in my word, you are truly my disciples, and you will know the truth, and the truth will make you free " (John 8:31). In his high-priestly prayer Jesus said concerning his disciples, " I have given them the words which thou gavest me, and they have received them and know in truth that I came from thee " (John 17:8). But even all of this instruction was not sufficient, therefore Jesus informed the disciples, " I have yet many things to say to you, but you cannot bear them now. When the Spirit of truth comes, he will guide you into all the truth " (John 16:12-13).

Without this preparatory instruction and the combination of signs and words at the cross, Christ's death would have been an enigma to the disciples. As it was they saw only dimly the meaning of reconciliation, and so the resurrected Christ continued his ministry of teaching and interpretation: for example, he opened the meaning of the Old Testament to the two men on the way to Emmaus. The apostles, especially Paul, had the conviction that through the aid of the Holy Spirit they had received further insight into the meaning of Christ's life, death, and resurrection. Thus, the church has traditionally accepted the whole New Testament as a witness to Christ.

When Jesus was challenged to select the great commandment in the law, he replied: " You shall love the Lord your God with all your heart, and with all your soul, and with all your mind. This is the great and first commandment. And a second is like it,

You shall love your neighbor as yourself. On these two commandments depend all the law and the prophets" (Matt. 22:37-40). Thus Jesus distilled the whole Old Testament down to two eternal truths, love for God and love for man. These commandments are propositional in form and certainly there has never been and never will be a time when these truths are not valid and applicable. Love, as Paul noted (I Cor. 13:13), is greater than faith and hope because it will be appropriate when the need for faith and hope has passed.

In spite of this fact, these and other teachings of Jesus are nonetheless objective truth. The only way to experience subjective truth is to be "in Christ," who said, "I am . . . the truth" (John 14:6). The words of Jesus are spirit and life, they are eternal, and they are indispensable for true faith, but they are mere words without the energizing and vitalizing influence of the Holy Spirit. Response can never become a reality by the sheer force of the written page. No doctrine, no matter how rationally and logically presented, can elicit true faith.

Scripture states, in clear propositional form, "God is love" (I John 4:8), but this truth is not the same as the timeless truth $2 \times 2 = 4$. Since human reason cannot discover and demonstrate that "God is love," many people have read this passage without coming to a subjective knowledge of its truth. While such lack of faith eliminates neither God nor the fact of his love, revelation never becomes a reality for those who do not believe—truth does not happen for them.

As further explanation concerning this kind of truth, Brunner states: "For our rational understanding of truth, this is an absurdity. Truth has nothing to do with 'happening'; truth 'is.' Truth is the agreement of something thought with something that exists. Such truth we can discover, and thus introduce it into time; but when it is known already this introduction into time becomes meaningless. A geometrical theorem was once discovered by someone for the first time; but since then this fact is of no interest so far as truth itself is concerned. The moment that it was perceived it became timeless. The truth of revelation is totally different, 'Grace and truth came by Jesus Christ.' This does not mean that they were discovered, so that all this now 'is' because it has been discovered. Rather, the knowledge of the truth remains permanently united with the historical process in which it came to us for the first time. The truth, the eternal Being and the eternal will of God, 'the mystery which hath been hid from ages and from generations now is made manifest to his saints.' But because it has been made manifest it has not become a 'static' truth. It is, and it remains, truth only for him who enters into that Event which is Jesus Christ, and remains there. It is always true only as something that 'happens,' as grace. Therefore 'grace and truth' belong indissolubly to one another." [25]

Although human reason can do its best to understand the statement "Jesus is Lord," the entire activity is within the realm of objective truth. This claim, which is propositional in form, remains a static truth until something "happens" in the realm of subjective truth. As Paul declares, "No one can say 'Jesus is Lord' except by the Holy Spirit" (I Cor. 12:3). On the other hand, this fact does not eliminate the objective phase which is preparatory to the Spirit's activity. Inasmuch as the Holy Spirit does not demand credulity, the leap of faith necessarily involves some consideration of the Lord to whom commitment is contemplated. As Brunner has stated, "Faith . . . must pass through an understanding of theological ideas, even if they are very simple ones."

Scripture, the objective record of revelation, sets forth its elemental ideas of God and Christ. If these are classified (in line with traditional categories) as doctrine, then a minimal core of doctrine is basic to genuine faith. But if, with Barth, Dodd, Baillie, and Brunner, "doctrine" is defined as a more or less elaborate, systematic body of teaching, then doctrine is the outgrowth, not the prerequisite, of faith. Herein, of course, lies some of the breakdown in communication between the two points of view. The essential point is that the objective truth of Scripture, whether defined in terms of doctrine or not, is the means by which the Holy Spirit leads to subjective truth.

While the means are necessary, God's ultimate purpose is that all men should enter the realm where grace, love, and truth become subjective realities. Paul depicts this process of re-creation as follows: "And we all, with unveiled face, beholding [or, reflecting] the glory of the Lord, are being changed into his likeness from one degree of glory to another; for this comes from the Lord who is the Spirit" (II Cor. 3:18). Paul recognized that teaching had a part to play, but his highest desire for his spiritual children was that they share in the revelation which occurs in subjective truth. Thus, in his prayer recorded in Eph. 3:14-19 he yearns that his readers may: (1) be strengthened in the inner man by the Holy Spirit; (2) have Christ dwelling in their hearts; (3) have power to comprehend the dimensions of love; (4) know the love of Christ, which surpasses knowledge; and (5) be filled with the fullness of God.

10: *Revelation, Inspiration, and Fact*

TRADITIONAL, conservative Christianity has viewed with alarm existentialism's broader definition of revelation and inspiration, and its claim that Scripture is objective or "it" truth, but these are not the issues that threaten the Christian faith. As noted previously, although these aspects of recent theological thought are different in formulation, they have root in Scripture, in the insights of Luther and Calvin, and in the experience of the church. The crucial issue is one's estimate of fact and history in Scripture. We have shown that some errors in minor details do not invalidate the trustworthy, historical basis for our faith. But can subjective truth become a reality if some of the key events of objective truth are in fact untrue?

Facts and Faith

The Old Testament writers never wearied of repeating the facts concerning God's gracious acts in behalf of Israel. Neither could they get away from the conviction that their God was back of so-called "human history." It is impossible to explain Israel's unique faith without acknowledging first that God did break into history and make himself known. In the Old Testament, therefore, it is beyond question that faith is rooted in fact.

This point of view is held with equal conviction in the New Testament. When the gnostic doctrine of the inherent sinfulness of matter and flesh began to creep into the early church, the incarnation had to be reinterpreted. Since Jesus of Nazareth was human, he could never be the Christ, the Son of God. Jesus appeared to be the Christ, but there was never any union of the two. Christ came down as a dove and clothed Jesus at his baptism. The New Testament writers were quick to recognize the fatal nature of this docetic view of Jesus. Accordingly, anyone who denied that Jesus Christ had come in the flesh had the "spirit of antichrist" (I John 4:2-3). Docetism not only necessitated a reinterpretation of the incarnation, it also had to deny the fact of the resurrection. Therefore, Paul is so bold as to affirm, "If Christ has not been raised, your faith is futile and you are still in your sins" (I Cor. 15:17).

Here, then, is the taproot of our faith, and here evangelical Christianity must take its stand. Docetism is still the enemy of the church — only its form has changed. Older liberalism thought in terms of objective history, and so in order to get around the historical problems in Scripture it separated facts and faith. Robert H. Pfeiffer (1892–1958), Old Testament scholar at Harvard, championed this view in all seriousness. He cited a number of interpretive sections in the historical books (e.g., Chronicles) and then showed how impossible it was to square the point of view expressed with the facts as learned from other portions of the Old Testament or from sources outside the Bible. Pfeiffer considered the attempt to combine faith with facts as "a snare and a delusion."[1] He justified his statement as follows: "Half measures, however, will not place Biblical research on a solid basis, on a par with research in other fields of the humanities, enjoying the full respect of competent scholars. The unhappy marriage of history and theology, owing to the prevalence of one over the other or else to mutual incompatibility, was never a true union and only divorce will result in the fruitful development of each of the two disciplines."[2] Near the close of his article Pfeiffer makes the sweeping statement, "Not only scholars, but even the humble untutored believers of all faiths intuitively know that facts and faith do not mix."[3]

History and Fact

Since the idea and meaning of the term "history" have exercised scholars and theologians greatly in the past few decades, these issues must be considered in our discussion of Biblical facts. It was popular at one time to speak of history as being objective, a simple reporting of the facts, while interpretation was thought of as being subjective, a matter of one's opinion or value judgment of an event. In time it was seen that no complex event or situation in life could be reported with *absolute* historical objectivity. In the first place, no historian ever had all the facts relating to his subject. Moreover, even from the available facts historians have been under the necessity of choosing which items to employ. It is evident that subjectivity is involved in such a process because the choice is determined by the mental and spiritual elements that characterize the historian. Thus, all history writing is a combination of subjective factors entwined with objective data.

This fact is equally true of Scripture. The Biblical writers mixed their faith and their history because their faith was a factor in recording the history. Herein lies the problem and the reason why varying forms of docetism have continued to this day. Pfeiffer took a more traditional view of history; therefore he interpreted the plain meaning of the text as the intent of the Old Testament writers. Thus, while frankly declaring that the writers were mistaken in many instances, he contended for the faith which Israel had.

On the other hand, the new Reformation theology and other contemporary theological developments have tended to solve the problem with a dual definition of history. Some find the key to the problem in Kierkegaard's "infinite qualitative difference" between time (man on earth) and eternity (God in heaven). This tremendous gap between the creator and his creatures means that revelation must come as God's vertical thrust into the historical realm of man. Revelation, therefore, can take place at only one point—the point of tangency being Jesus Christ. The claim in John 1:14, "the Word became flesh," must be maintained, accordingly, at all costs. God entered, in a very objective manner, the space-time categories of man's existence, but this act was not essentially a part of the running stream of history. Rather, it was "primal history" (*Urgeschichte*) breaking into human history. This concept of a history above history, a "superhistory," involves some neat juggling of *time* and *eternity* in which the two are related "dialectically."

Rudolf Bultmann approaches the historical problem with two different sets of German words: (1) *historisch,* "historical"—an event (*Historie*) that lies wholly in the past, and (2) *geschichtlich,* "historic"—an event (*Geschichte*) that has existential meaning for the present and possibly lies in the past as well. We come to know these differing events in two quite different ways—the "historical" by the common methods of research into human history and the "historic" by means of personal encounter. *Historie* gives meaningless facts; only *Geschichte* can give meaning.

H. P. Owen in *Revelation and Existence,* a study of Bultmann's theology, explains the subtle difference as follows: "The nerve of the distinction is the difference between two views of history's relationship to time. An 'historical' event is wholly temporal. Its nature and significance are exhausted by the stretch of time that it occupies. An 'historic' event, *the* historic event of Jesus Christ, is not wholly temporal; it is both temporal and eternal; it is the point at which eternity crosses time. Christ was a temporal figure, as much a temporal figure as Socrates or Julius Caesar; but the Word that God spoke through him was an eternal Word; therefore this Word can be renewed in each encounter."[4] Because the Bible is written in "historical" terms, Bultmann considers it obsolete and incapable of revealing the personal God in any effective, personal way. It has many passages which (while intelligible and capable of being understood) have no significance or application to modern life. These "meaningless" elements Bultmann calls "myth," and the process of reinterpretation he calls "demythologization."

John's doctrine of "the Word" as a being "with God" Bultmann reinterprets to mean "the Word of address" which the Father speaks. Christ as the incarnation of God becomes Jesus the human figure through whom the Word is spoken. Jesus' death on the cross is God speaking his Word of forgiveness.

One of the chief categories to be demythologized is miracles. Miracle stories are "myth" because they picture God's act as an object that draws the attention of the reader. When God reveals himself in personal encounter with man the act of disclosure must be concealed. It can never be demonstrated or proved by objective evidence. Therefore, the reinterpretation of Scripture must do away with all objective, historical elements. Faith must come from an inner revelation, person to person, not an appeal to external facts of past history.

What, then, does Bultmann do with the resurrection? Owen observes: "Bultmann is here faced with a difficulty. In the Incarnation and the Cross he had two indubitable historical events (a man and the death of a man) which he could demythologize, but, in his view, the Resurrection was not an historical event at all. His presuppositions are such that he is bound to assert that it could never have happened. Yet surely something happened, on the basis of which the New Testament accounts of the Resurrection-appearances were composed. Bultmann is prepared to admit that there was something — perhaps 'a series of subjective visions' — but he regards anything of this kind that may have happened as completely irrelevant to Christian faith. Nevertheless, a demythologized Resurrection must be connected with *some* historical event if it is to have the slightest credibility. This historical event is the Cross. To believe in the risen Christ is to believe that through the Cross God forgives our sins and frees us for 'newness of life.' This is the only sense in which it can be said that God through Christ 'brought life and immortality to light.' 'The faith of Easter is just this — faith in the Word of preaching.'"[5]

In contrast to Bultmann's frank denial of the resurrection, Barth has expressed the conviction that anyone who denies the resurrection of Christ is not a Christian. But Barth's belief in the resurrection must be understood in the light of his view of history. He, like Bultmann, distinguishes between *Historie* and *Geschichte.* The fact that he has not defined these terms precisely, and that he considers the resurrection as *Geschichte,* not *Historie,* has raised doubts as to whether he really believes the resurrection occurred as an actual historical event in chronological time. Richard R. Niebuhr contends that Barth's concept of history forces him "to extrude the resurrection event from the sequence that anchors it in the New Testament." [6]

The Cruciality of Facts

In apparent contradiction to Bultmann and Barth, Brunner states: "Biblical theology is not only a theology of the Word, but also of facts, and it is true of such facts which are at the same time the object of historical research. The article of the Creed, 'Crucified under Pontius Pilate,' reminds us of this. It forms part of the 'offense' of the Christian faith that, in contrast to mysticism or to rational moralistic theism, it is connected with historic facts, which are the object of historical research." [7] He also expresses a fear that Bultmann and Barth are in danger of making Christianity into a form of docetism with timeless ideas; therefore he comments: "Another effort to evade this difficulty has been to depreciate the fact, in comparison with the 'given Word.' The Word has been given to us; the facts that lie behind it do not concern us; all we have to inquire into is the meaning of the Word, not whether the facts actually took place. This position, however, contains a docetic tendency which is just as dangerous, and indeed at bottom still more dangerous, than docetism in the usual Christological sense. Only if Jesus Christ actually, in the sense of a historical fact which took place within time and space, was crucified upon the hill of Calvary, can he be our Redeemer. The question, What is told us? cannot be separated from that other question, What has happened? for what we are told is precisely that this event has actually happened." [8]

But Brunner's concern for facts is conditioned by the critical question with which he examines each concrete event recorded in the Bible: "Are there any results or truths of historical science that contradict the statements of the Christian faith? Thus, does the faith assert 'facts' whose actual historicity can be denied or contested by historical research?"[9] As R. R. Niebuhr declares: "Consequently, when he comes to the interpretation of the resurrection of Jesus — the central and crucial element in the whole 'fact' of Jesus Christ, according to Brunner — he is not in a position to give it any more of a footing in history than did his predecessors. The resurrection cannot be called a fact, he believes; rather it is a superhistorical or eschatological happening and 'no longer historical at all.' The resurrection is a 'hole' in history, of which only the edges are historical. Shining through that hole, faith sees ineffable eternity. The assumption of Brunner's thought, here and elsewhere, is that history is the facade or mask behind which true meaning is concealed."[10]

Brunner is careful to protect the historicity of Jesus and his death on the cross because there is no redemption apart from this event. Paul, however, goes farther and affirms that if Christ has not been raised, then all of us are still in our sins (I Cor. 15:17). Evidently the offense and scandal of the gospel includes the resurrection as well as the death on the cross. Brunner is certainly correct in his concern over those who "depreciate the fact," but does he not indict himself when he depreciates the *ultimate fact?*

Another area of disagreement among scholars is the doctrine of the virgin birth of Christ. Some who believe in the historical life of Jesus draw the line with this doctrine. They point out, quite accurately, that aside from Matt. 1:18-25 and Luke 1:28-35 no other portion of the New Testament makes reference to this doctrine. Paul, Peter, and John had numerous occasions to refer to it, but they pass it by. Obviously, the doctrine was not an issue in the beginnings of Christianity, and most important of all, it was not an essential element of the gospel as preached from Pentecost on. Accordingly, they reject the doctrine as non-essential to their salvation.

It is interesting that Barth, whom Brunner questions in other issues, takes Brunner to task for his negative attitude toward the virgin birth of Christ. Commenting on Brunner's *The Mediator,* Barth quotes Berdyaev as expressing his own views: "I read Brunner's book with tremendous interest, because I felt in him tenseness and acuity of thought, religious sensibility. But when I reached the passage in which Brunner confesses that he does not believe in Jesus Christ's birth of the Virgin, or at least confronts it with indifference, my mood became sad and the matter grew tedious. For it seemed to me as though everything had now been canceled, as though everything else was now pointless."[11]

With respect to this doctrine C. S. Lewis states: "I can understand the man who denies miracles altogether: but what is one to make of people who will believe other miracles and 'draw the line' at the Virgin Birth? . . . In reality the Miracle is no less, and no more, surprising than any others."[12]

The concern of Barth, Berdyaev, and Lewis raises the question as to the cruciality of this doctrine. In his book *The Virgin Birth of Christ,* J. Gresham Machen (1881–1937) comments as follows on this issue: "Is belief in the virgin birth necessary to every man if he is to be a believer in the Lord Jesus Christ? The question is wrongly put when it is put in that way. Who can tell exactly how much knowledge of the facts about Christ is necessary if a man is to have saving faith? None but God can tell. Some knowledge is certainly required, but exactly how much is required we cannot say. 'Lord, I believe; help thou mine unbelief,' said a man in the Gospels who was saved. So today there are many men of little faith, many who are troubled by the voices that are heard on all sides. It is very hard to be a Christian in these times; and there is One who knows that it is hard. What right have we to say that full knowledge and full conviction are necessary before a man can put his trust in the crucified and risen Lord? What right have we to say that no man can be saved before he has come to full conviction regarding the stupendous miracle narrated in the first chapters of Matthew and Luke?"[13] Lest he be misunderstood, however, Machen adds, "We do not mean by what we have just said that denial of the virgin birth is to be treated as a matter of indifference by the wise pastor of souls."[14] Then he concludes, "One thing at least is clear: even if the belief in the virgin birth is not necessary to every Christian, it is certainly necessary to Christianity. And it is necessary to the corporate witness of the church."[15]

Facts and Christian Dynamic

Machen has shown the impossibility of prescribing a minimal core of Biblical events to which assent must be given before saving faith is possible. God recognizes the sincere doubts of men and he undoubtedly saves men who do not have enough faith to believe certain teachings of Scripture. But the question is how long an individual, or the church, can continue with these doubts and still have the power of the Holy Spirit. Does there not come a time when one must rise to new levels of faith and insight or else grieve the Spirit whose task it is to witness to all the truths concerning Christ?

If one employs no other criterion than the pragmatic test of twentieth-century church history, the answer seems to be in the affirmative. As a general rule, churches with ministers and leaders who have consistently denied, or at least minimized, the doctrines of the virgin birth and the resurrection of Jesus Christ have tended to lose the sense of mission. The call to sacrifice and personal commitment becomes so weak that there is no strength to bring forth spiritual children. Therefore, many of these congregations have to go back twenty-five to fifty years to find the record of the last person who entered the full-time Christian ministry.

History and Interpretation

The Christian faith as set forth in Scripture is a combination of deed and word, event and interpretation. As a general rule, therefore, pessimism concerning the actual historicity of events recorded in the Bible is also accompanied by doubts concerning the genuineness and validity of the teachings attributed to Jesus. The best current example is Bultmann, who is one of the most extreme scholars of the *Formgeschichte* (form history, known popularly in America as form criticism) school of New Testament interpretation. According to him, few, if any, of the words attributed to Jesus derived from him. Rather, they were the ideas of the expanding church, which sought to express its faith in this manner.

In opposition to this view, W. F. Albright comments: "Form critics are no doubt correct in emphasizing the practical role which the Gospels played in the early church, a role which may well account in part for the survival of certain traditions at the expense of others. This, however, is very different from the highly subjective and improbable view which form-critics usually hold, that much of the content of the Gospels was adapted or even invented to suit situations which arose in the life of the church. In other words, most form critics suppose that the Gospels reflect the life of the subapostolic church as against the traditional view that the Gospels are original documents antedating the subapostolic church. Archaeological data already speak with no uncertain voice against the vagaries of radical form criticism according to Dibelius, and even more decisively against the extreme views of some of his followers. The Gospel of John is in a peculiarly vulnerable position, against which Bultmann, in particular, has carried on an unremitting campaign for decades. John is supposed by these scholars to contain virtually no original historical matter, but to reflect an early second-century Christian group tinged more than a little by gnosticism."[16]

In another context Albright shows that the discovery of early Greek manuscripts of the Gospel of John, the appearance of the gnostic documents at Chenoboskion, Egypt (1946), the discovery of the Dead Sea (Qumrân) scrolls in 1947 and the following years, and archaeological confirmation of specific details in the Gospel of John all indicate that the oral tradition of this Gospel account goes back prior to the fall of Jerusalem in A.D. 70.[17]

Albright concurs heartily with James A. Montgomery (1866–1949), who concluded that "the Gospel of St. John is the composition of a well-informed Jew, not of the Pharisaic party, whose life experience was gained in Palestine in the first half of the first century, and whose mother tongue was Aramaic; and that this conclusion alone explains the excellence of the historical data and the philological phenomena of the book."[18] It is strange, indeed, if an account that includes some precise data about Palestine and Jerusalem prior to A.D. 70 does not preserve corresponding theological accuracy and authenticity. There is every reason, therefore, for considering the discourses of John's Gospel as accurate insights into the meaning of authentic statements made by Jesus.

However, this conclusion should not be construed as an argument in support of the extreme view which holds that every word attributed to Jesus in the Gospels is an exact, almost stenographic, report of his sayings. At least two features militate against this view: (1) the extant Greek text is a translation of the original statements made in Aramaic, and (2) the marked difference between the words of Jesus in the Synoptics and in John indicates that some later insights of the apostolic tradition have been read back into the accounts. Nevertheless, these interpretations with respect to the person and teachings of Jesus have their root in his earthly ministry. In Albright's opinion "there is scarcely a passage in the Gospels which was appreciably influenced in form by the history of the church in the decades immediately following the year A.D. 70."[19]

Accordingly, the Biblical and non-Biblical data warrant a mediating position between the optimism of the old stenographic view and the pessimism of Bultmann. The evangelical church must not be guilty of a credulity that refuses to use its reason.

It would do well to accept Luther's basic assumption, "Christ is Lord and King of Scripture." Where Scripture, "the crib wherein Christ lies," cannot stand the test of incontrovertible evidence, the church must admit it. On the other hand, the church must not succumb to the pressures of our scientific world in those areas where humble men of science do not presume to speak with finality.

Notwithstanding all the problems associated with Scripture, the only Christ the church knows is the Christ of the New Testament, the Christ seen through the eyes of the apostles. At all costs we must steer a course between two extremes. In one instance the church has stressed the inerrancy of the Bible to such an extent that some people have limited salvation to those who first hold correct views with respect to the teachings of Scripture. Yet it is plainly evident from the history of the church that a correct understanding of the objective truth in Scripture can never guarantee an experience of personal, subjective truth. Submission to Christ is primarily a matter of decision, an exercise of our will, not knowledge.

The other extreme to be avoided is the belief that a person can maintain genuine faith in Christ while doubting the truth and relevance of much that Scripture declares. The will to believe cannot be effective for long when it reckons much of the objective truth of Scripture as untrue. The power of the Holy Spirit does not become a reality until one responds to the Christ of Scripture. As in the case of Biblical events, so in the matter of interpretation, where churches discount the essential teachings of Scripture, leanness of soul is sure to follow. If the church is to experience the revelation and inspiration of God, it must return with a spirit of humility and obedience to God's record of revelation in the Bible.

11: *Inerrancy, Doctrine, Security, and Authority*

INASMUCH as previous discussion of doctrine was more in the context of issues posed by recent theological thought, it is necessary to consider in some detail the aspects of doctrine that relate primarily to the concept of inerrancy. As observed in earlier chapters, some evangelical scholars are inclined to treat the teaching and the phenomena of Scripture in the light of the deductive premise that God, if he were truly God, had to reveal himself inerrantly. This concern to protect God's honor is rooted, quite obviously, in the doctrine of divine sovereignty. It is no accident, then, that some of these same scholars are so bold as to declare, "It is only the followers of Calvin who have a theology that fully fits in with this idea of Scripture."[1] Could it be that their doctrine of inspiration derives from this theology which is read back into Scripture?

Inerrancy and Sovereignty

The sovereignty of God is a crucial doctrine, indeed, for if God is not sovereign, we as Christians are engaged in a hopeless struggle. Essentially, sovereignty means the authority and power to achieve a desired goal. Yet one can believe that God is going to achieve his purpose with mankind and still recognize that God is not restricted to one unalterable method in attaining this goal. Is the most sovereign God the one who must always act in a prescribed way because his nature permits no other, or is he the one who can work in a variety of ways in order that a greater purpose be achieved?

All Christians accept the truth of Num. 23:19: "God is not man, that he should lie," but all of Scripture does not come under the category of supernatural revelation. Because God did not override some Biblical writers in their use of erroneous sources does not mean that God is a liar. He can hardly be charged with the defects of the human instruments and their sources.

But the view of sovereignty held by some conservatives does not permit this distinction and so they feel constrained to plead for God's honor in every detail. "Why insist on verbal inspiration," it is asked, "when no one can produce the documents that are to be regarded as thus inspired? . . . If the theory is true, then we would dishonor God if we held any other. Surely, we would not want to do that!"[2] But when the Biblical data disprove this theory how is God honored by it?

The fervor with which some Christians cling to this strict view of sovereignty is illustrated by the following statement: "God, we are being told, had to use the means at his disposal. Those means were human beings. Therefore, when God revealed his Word, that Word, in passing through the media of human writers, acquired the characteristics of those writers, including their error, their ignorance, their crudities. Well may we exclaim at the poverty and weakness of such a God! If indeed man can thus thwart him, it is pertinent to ask, Is he really worth knowing after all?"[3] God did not have to use human beings — he chose to do so. In this choice God was showing anything but "poverty and weakness," and in no instance has man really thwarted God. In another context we read: "God has revealed to us his Word. What are we to think of him if this Word is glutted with little annoying inaccuracies? Why could not the omnipotent and omniscient God have taken the trouble to give us a Word that was free from error? Was it not a somewhat discourteous thing for him to have breathed forth from his mouth a message filled with mistakes? Of course, it was discourteous; it was downright rude and insulting. The present writer finds it difficult to have much respect for such a God."[4] Dare one say that God was "rude and insulting" when he determined to use human instrumentality in the giving, transmitting, and the translating of his revelation? This process was intended to honor both God and man. For the good of his ultimate goal God has accepted willingly the "little annoying inaccuracies" even though they plague some of those who love him and would defend his honor.

Concerning this doctrine of sovereignty, Llewelyn J. Evans comments: "God has not so poised the Rock of Ages that the Higher or Lower Criticism, with pickax or crowbar, digging out a chronological inaccuracy here, or prying off a historical contradiction there, is going to upset it. The critic may be all right, the crowbar may be all right, but the Rock of Ages is all right too, and it will stand fast forever. Do not, I beseech you, charge upon God the priggish precision which makes as much of a molehill as of a mountain. God does not care to be honored in that way."[5]

There is a high correlation between a deterministic definition of sovereignty and the doctrine of inerrancy. Although some Christians may hold the latter without the former, almost without exception those who believe in a strict view of sovereignty also contend for the doctrine of inerrancy. This view of inspiration is often characterized as the "high view of inspiration," the implication being that "high" means "best" or "true." Is one justified, however, in claiming more than Scripture does? Can there be in actuality a higher view than the Biblical view?

With respect to the danger of trying to prove too much, Paul K. Jewett acknowledges, "The theologian must never attempt to speak more plainly than God."[6] In more expanded form, James I. Packer affirms: "The humble pupil of Scripture will . . . not be so self-willed as, on the one hand, to build a speculative theological system which will say more about God than God has said about himself, or, on the other, to ignore or tone down what Scripture does say because he finds it hard to fit in with the rest of what he knows. His aim is to learn all that God teaches, and give it all its due place in his own thought. And he will never let himself suppose that now he has finished learning and knows everything; instead, he will keep listening to Scripture for further correction and instruction."[7]

These two warnings are well taken. Unless the attitude expressed becomes a characteristic of Christians everywhere, there will be no hope of healing the wounds that enervate the vitality of the church. But being instructed and corrected by the clear evidence at hand means putting our theory into practice regardless of the cost.

Inerrancy and Salvation

The doctrine of inspiration has loomed so large and taken up so much of the thought of certain groups within Protestantism during the last seventy-five years that it has tended to become the pivotal doctrine of the gospel. In many quarters, in fact, popular opinion assumes that Christian faith is impossible without belief in the inerrancy of Scripture. Warfield, however, made it quite clear that Christianity and salvation are not primarily dependent on inerrancy. He declared: "Let it not be said that thus we found the whole Christian system upon the doctrine of plenary inspiration. We found the whole Christian system on the doctrine of plenary inspiration as little as we found it upon the doctrine of angelic existences. Were there no such thing as inspiration, Christianity would be true, and all its essential doctrines would be credibly witnessed to us in the generally trustworthy reports of the teaching of our Lord and of his authoritative agents in founding the church, preserved in the writings of the apostles and their first followers, and in the historical witness of the living church. Inspiration is not the most fundamental of Christian doctrines, nor even the first thing we prove about the Scriptures. It is the last and crowning fact as to the Scriptures. These we first prove authentic, historically credible, generally trustworthy, before we prove them inspired."[8]

Warfield expressed himself even more forcibly as follows: "We are in entire harmony in this matter with what we conceive to be the very true statement recently made by Dr. George P. Fisher, that 'if the authors of the Bible were credible reporters of revelations of God, whether in the form of historical transactions of which they were witnesses, or of divine mysteries that were unveiled to their minds, their testimony would be entitled to belief, even if they were shut up to their unaided faculties in communicating what they had thus received.' We are in entire sympathy in this matter therefore, with the protest which Dr. Marcus Dods raised in his famous address at the meeting of the Alliance of the Reformed Churches at London, against representing that 'the infallibility of the Bible is the ground of the whole Christian faith.' We judge with him that it is very important indeed that such a misapprehension, if it is anywhere current, should be corrected." [9] Notwithstanding this warning, it is not uncommon in some Christian circles today for people to consider as unchristian any person who has the courage to speak out against inerrancy. Apparently the views of Warfield noted above have not been propagated as thoroughly as has his doctrine of inspiration. We would do well to heed Carl F. H. Henry when he declares, "The question is not whether one's theory of inspiration is a saving truth; it is not." [10]

Inerrancy and Doctrine

If, as all evangelical leaders now acknowledge, the doctrine of inerrancy is not necessary for salvation, why is this view of inspiration considered so vital? The basic reason is doctrine. According to this argument, if the doctrine of inerrancy is given up, all confidence in the Biblical writers as trustworthy witnesses to doctrine is undermined. If they prove to be wrong in their claim of inerrancy, where are they trustworthy? But this line of reasoning is nothing more than "False in one, false in all" applied to the area of doctrine. There are other choices than the either-or presented by this argument.

Take, for example, the problem of Jesus' view of inspiration. We have seen how he and the New Testament writers referred, either explicitly or implicitly, to the manuscripts of the Old Testament current in their day. These were errant, as all are compelled to admit, so the dilemma arises. We are told that we must believe either (1) that Jesus taught inerrancy, or (2) that he was fanatical or dishonest. But all of this stems from the assumption that Jesus taught inerrancy. If he believed what the doctrine of inerrancy claims for him, then he was indeed fanatical or dishonest because he did support his theory in practice.

But why must one start with the assumption of inerrancy? The inductive evidence of the New Testament indicates that Jesus taught a strong doctrine of inspiration and authority of Scripture, yet without claiming inerrancy. Once this is recognized, there is no need to discredit Jesus by considering him either a fanatic or a liar.

The threat that denial of inerrancy supposedly poses for doctrine is also expressed in the equation: fallible history = fallible doctrine. It is nonsense, so it is claimed, to speak of fallible history in the Bible and then affirm that it has infallible doctrine. Accordingly, since the Christian faith is rooted in history, it is necessary to contend for inerrancy both in history and in doctrine. The writer has no quarrel on the issue of history's being vital to faith. As noted previously, facts and faith are complementary and mutually dependent. But minor historical errors in Scripture invalidate neither our faith nor true doctrine. This leads us, therefore, to consider whether proven historical errors mean that Scripture also contains some fallible elements in doctrine.

One of the important passages in the New Testament is Jesus' discourse on the Mount of Olives (Matt. 24:1-42; Mark, ch. 13; Luke 21:5-36). Concerning the buildings of the Temple area, Jesus said, "Truly, I say to you, there will not be left here one stone upon another, that will not be thrown down." According to Mark and Luke the disciples inquire as to when "these things" will happen. Their question seems to refer to the destruction of Jerusalem. Luke makes this explicit, for in ch. 21:20 we read, "But when you see Jerusalem surrounded by armies, then know that its desolation has come near." Luke 21:24 also states, "And Jerusalem will be trodden down by the Gentiles, until the times of the Gentiles are fulfilled."

In Matt. 24:3, however, the disciples are reported as saying, "Tell us, when will this be, and what will be the sign of your coming and of the close of the age?" Matt. 24:14 makes reference to the "end," and in ch. 24:27 "the coming of the Son of man" is likened to "lightning." Accordingly, Matthew's account implies that the disciples related Christ's second coming and the close of the age to the destruction of the Temple. Moreover, in a discussion about the tribulations that were to come, Mark 13:10 notes, "And the gospel must first be preached to all nations." Thus Matthew and Mark bring in matters that clearly refer to Christ's second coming.

Yet after the parable of the fig tree Jesus is reported as saying, "Truly, I say to you, this generation will not pass away till all these things take place." With the exception that Luke omits "these," the text of this verse is identical in all three Gospels. There would be no problem here if the passage referred only to the destruction of Jerusalem in A.D. 70, but what is one to do with the preceding and following verses which refer clearly to Christ's second coming? The normal way out of the difficulty for conservatives has been to reinterpret the Greek word *genea,* "generation," as meaning something else than the people living in Jesus' day. Some have interpreted "this generation" as referring to the generation that was to see the signs at the close of the age. Others have felt that the expression refers to the unconverted world (for example, Paul's reference to the "perverse generation" in Phil. 2:15). Still others, interpreting "generation" to mean "race," have inferred that Jesus was referring to the Jews.

While these interpretations may answer the problem for some twentieth-century Christians, none of them takes into account the difficulty that the disciples faced. In this same discourse

Jesus warns them about being led astray by "false Christs and false prophets." Matthew 24:36 has the additional warning, "But of that day and hour no one knows, not even the angels of heaven, nor the Son, but the Father only." This statement would seem to imply a longer period of waiting, yet there is plenty of Biblical evidence to show that the early church expected Christ to return in its day. Would Christ speak to his disciples in such ambiguous terms that they would interpret *genea* literally while he had some hidden meaning whereby he was allowing for many centuries before his return? Is it not more likely that the disciples confused some of Jesus' statements about the destruction of Jerusalem with some of his remarks about his second coming? But whether the difficulty lay in the original statement of Jesus or the interpretation of the disciples, it certainly existed in the original copies of the Gospels. Although it is difficult to give conclusive proof of contradiction, some of the verses noted in the three Gospels were in all likelihood inserted out of context, and, accordingly, they constitute erroneous elements of doctrine.

Christ's personal return is clearly taught in the New Testament, yet this fact hardly necessitates the view that the Biblical writers saw eye to eye in all the doctrinal details related to eschatology. The conservative assumption has been that every bit of evidence having anything to do with "end times" has its place in some vast eschatological chart which, not unlike a jigsaw puzzle, was revealed by God to the Biblical writers piece by piece. The task of the interpreter, according to this view, is to correlate all the Scriptural references to "that day," "the day of the Lord," "the day of judgment," *parousia, apocalypse, epiphany,* and *millennium,* with the expectation that the true picture will emerge when all the pieces have been correctly placed. Is it not a significant fact that all the brains and ingenuity of Christianity have been frustrated in this attempt to get a unified, clear picture? Is there not something wrong in the exchange of charge and countercharge where each interpretation claims the personal aid of the Holy Spirit in arriving at the so-called "Biblical doctrine of eschatology"?

This apparent diversity of doctrinal data is also evident in other areas of theology, for example, the atonement of Christ. There are many views, but none of them incorporates all the Biblical evidence in its systematic formulation. The clear meaning of some passages does not fit in with the clear meaning of others. Christian theologians have worked diligently and long in attempts to arrange all the contents of Scripture, God's seed-plot of objective truth, into one consistent pattern, but no system of theology has achieved this goal. The usual explanation is that the Biblical diversity is not really contradiction, but paradox (apparent contradiction), and that someday when our mortal minds put on immortality we will have the answers to all the difficulties in Scripture. Can we, however, really attribute all our problems to faulty interpretation? Is it not equally possible that details of doctrine tend to get fuzzy as one nears the fringes of truth?

This does not mean, on the other hand, that the Biblical writers are not trustworthy guides in the area of doctrine. The claim that one error in doctrine undercuts the whole basis for any assurance in doctrine is not valid. This, as noted previously, is the misconception "False in one, false in all." We can be sure that the Biblical writers were just as consistent and accurate in the realms of faith, morals, and doctrine as they were in the area of history.

But this fact leads eventually to the question, "What is to be the standard for determining trustworthy and authoritative doctrine?" According to the New Testament writers, Christ and the gospel are determinative. To those who doubted that deity would ever have come in the form of human flesh John declared, "By this you know the Spirit of God: every spirit which confesses that Jesus Christ has come in the flesh is of God, and every spirit which does not confess Jesus is not of God" (I John 4:2-3). The denial of the incarnation was "the spirit of antichrist." To the Corinthians who doubted the resurrection of the dead Paul affirmed, "If Christ has not been raised, then our preaching is in vain and your faith is in vain" (I Cor. 15:14). The Biblical writers shared unequivocally some doctrines that cluster around Jesus, the incarnate Christ, and the way of salvation.

This is evident from the preaching of the apostles in The Acts and Paul's declaration in Gal. 1:6-9: "I am astonished that you are so quickly deserting him who called you in the grace of Christ and turning to a different gospel — not that there is another gospel, but there are some who trouble you and want to pervert the gospel of Christ. But even if we, or an angel from heaven, should preach to you a gospel contrary to that which we preached to you, let him be accursed. As we have said before, so now I say again, If any one is preaching to you a gospel contrary to that which you received, let him be accursed." For most Christians today the *kerygma,* "preaching, proclamation," of the New Testament writers concerning the "gospel of Christ" is still the authoritative standard for doctrinal formulations. The time-honored Apostles' Creed, which contains most of the *kerygma,* continues to be repeated as a summary of the essential doctrines of the Christian faith.

But when the Biblical writers move away from basic doctrinal statements and attempt to delineate some details of these doctrines there is generally less uniformity of teaching. The valid procedure, so it would appear, is to accept the view that accounts for the most Biblical data related to the subject. This decision tends to become increasingly difficult, of course, as the Biblical evidence becomes more evenly distributed. It is imperative, therefore, that Christians have a genuine inclination to "live and let live" in the ambiguous areas of doctrine. All Biblical doctrine is not infallible, but it is sufficiently accurate as a whole to achieve the goal that God desires.

Inerrancy and the Incarnation

Another prominent argument for inerrancy stems from the analogy of Scripture to Christ. Just as the incarnate Word was human and yet sinless, so the written word, coming through human channels, is errorless. Warfield, for example, accepts this conclusion, but he does so with some reservations. He declares: "But the analogy with our Lord's Divine-human personality may easily be pressed beyond reason. There is no hypostatic union between the Divine and the human in Scripture; we cannot parallel the 'inscripturation' of the Holy Spirit and the incarnation of the Son of God. The Scriptures are merely the product of Divine and human forces working together to produce a product in the production of which the human forces work under the initiation and prevalent direction of the Divine: the person of our Lord unites in itself Divine and human natures, each of which retains its distinctness while operating only in relation to the other. Between such diverse things there can exist only a remote analogy; and, in point of fact, the analogy in the present instance amounts to no more than that in both cases Divine and human factors are involved, though very differently. In the one they unite to constitute a Divine-human person, in the other they cooperate to perform a Divine-human work."[11] It is precisely this unique, once-only union of the human and the divine in Christ which makes it different from the blending of divine and human elements in Scripture. The Bible is the record of God's revelation. Indeed, it resulted from God's initiative working through human instrumentality, but it came into existence over a long period of time involving hundreds of sources of information, writers, and scribes.

Furthermore, language, as we have seen, cannot completely express or contain all the factors in human personality. How much less can it do so with the wider scope of divine personality! Paul did not, and most certainly would not, say that "the whole fullness of deity dwells" in the written word. Somehow, and this is a mystery too, human personality is capable of expressing more of deity than is human language. For this reason the rigid analogy between Christ and the Bible breaks down. One can hold to a belief in the sinlessness of Christ and still accept Scripture as being fallible in minor details.

The fear implicit in the various objections to admitting some error, both historical and doctrinal, is unwarranted. God is still working through the Holy Spirit to give conviction concerning the truth of his written word. It is a trustworthy record of God's teaching (doctrine), and therefore, as Paul informs us, it will always be profitable for teaching. In the basic matters that are repeated time and again, and that are woven throughout the Bible, one can speak with assurance, but once the Christian interpreter leaves the central path of doctrine he must be less dogmatic because the fringes shade off. In brief, then, the sovereignty of God, the honor of Jesus Christ, and the trustworthiness of Biblical doctrine are not at stake in accepting a view of inspiration that rejects the qualification of inerrancy.

Inerrancy and Security

Notwithstanding the evidence that has been presented, some concerns of those who cherish the doctrine of inerrancy have not yet been answered satisfactorily. One of these has to do with the proverbial "camel." If one error is admitted, then the camel gets his nose in the tent and soon there is more of him, and finally he occupies the whole tent. This is a genuine fear for many Christians. While history teaches us the validity of concern at this point, it also shows us that this is only one side of the danger.

Too often the person who believes in inerrancy forgets that his personal experience is beset with many temptations and pitfalls. He needs to be reminded that the closer one comes in fellowship with God the more subtle the temptations become. There is no security outside of daily commitment of oneself as a living sacrifice to God. Creeds cannot protect. The one who holds to inerrancy is in as grave danger as the person who rejects the doctrine.

It is also quite futile to talk of "running from evil." We need to recognize that wherever the genuine is, the counterfeit will be found too. In the doctrine of the Trinity, for example, truth and error are separated only by a fine line. If one runs from the error, one is also running from the truth. This is so in all of our spiritual experience. The Christian life is difficult and requires the wisdom and strength of the Holy Spirit. Only in this way can the church maintain its integrity. It must seek the truth, and yet while doing so, it will constantly be in danger of evil. How grateful we should be, then, for the Biblical assurance that one can be in the world of evil and yet not of it.

In the eternal quest for security in the Christian life, the usual warning is, "Stay on the right-hand side of the road." This is no solution to the problem either, for as Bernard Ramm points out, "We can sin to the right as well as to the left."[12] This possibility has not come into the consciousness of many Christians, and as a result they tend to be left-eyed. While seeing the dangers on their left hand, they are oblivious to equal or greater dangers on the right. In the area of doctrine a person can postulate too much. The history of theology is replete with examples of "superbelief," a creed beyond that set forth by Scripture. As noted earlier, however, one is hardly honoring God by believing things of him or his will which are not true.

Inerrancy and Apostasy

A major contention of those who hold to inerrancy is that once a person leaves the security of inerrancy he will eventually swing to the opposite side and become an extreme liberal. There have been numerous examples of this transition during the last century or so. In fact, some of the most radical liberals have been men who have had evangelical background and convictions, but because of the rigidity with which they were restrained previously they reacted violently when confronted in college or university with the other side of the problems.

This was to be expected, of course, since in the early stages of the struggle between traditionalism and liberalism the alternatives consisted mainly of the two extremes. But during the last fifty years the pendulum has settled down and there has emerged a mediating attitude toward Scripture and theology. Many Christians have maintained a warm, vital faith with deep concern for Scripture while at the same time recognizing the untenable nature of the doctrine of inerrancy. The person who claims that history proves "loss of inerrancy = liberalism" has not investigated all the evidence.

Inerrancy as Protection

A clear verdict of history, on the other hand, is the futility of man's attempt to protect himself and his doctrine. Every attempt has failed sooner or later. The Jewish rabbis said, "Make a fence around the Torah." In order to protect the law of Moses they elaborated hundreds of rules to alert an individual before he could break the law. Yet Jew after Jew, Paul included, had the experience of being driven forward by his human nature until Moses' law had been broken.

There is no absolute protection against doctrinal deviation. God has not deemed such rigid precautions necessary. Even in the Garden of Eden, with his whole creative plan at stake, God put no other barrier between Adam and Eve and "the tree of the knowledge of good and evil" than his personal prohibition. God took the greatest risk possible.

The only protection God has provided is the Holy Spirit's working dynamically in a committed heart, mind, and body. This is sufficient protection for salvation, but it is still not certain protection against false doctrine. Take, for example, the case of Philip Mauro. As a converted lawyer he devoted his talents to the cause of Christ. He was one of the writers in *The Fundamentals,* the series of twelve volumes published from 1909 to 1911. By 1913 he went into print favoring dispensationalism and the pretribulation rapture of the church. Fifteen years later he published *The Gospel of the Kingdom,* in which he repudiated all his dispensational views. As George E. Ladd observes, "Among the reasons was the sudden realization that the Scofield Bible 'has usurped the place of authority that belongs to God's

Bible alone.'"[13] Ladd quotes Mauro further as saying: "It is mortifying to remember that I not only held and taught these novelties myself, but that I even enjoyed a complacent sense of superiority because thereof, and regarded with feelings of pity and contempt those who had not received the 'new light' and were unacquainted with this up-to-date method of 'rightly dividing the word of truth.' . . . The time came . . . when the inconsistencies and self-contradictions of the system itself, and above all, the impossibility of reconciling its main positions with the plain statement of the Word of God, became so glaringly evident that I could not do otherwise than to renounce it."[14] Neither Mauro's view of inspiration nor the presence of the Holy Spirit in his life protected him from the doctrine that necessitated his "mortifying" experience.

Inerrancy as a Barrier

From beginning to end, history warns us that theological Maginot lines or fences fail to achieve their purpose. Not only do they fail to protect, but they also *restrict* the outreach of the truth being guarded. This is the ultimate tragedy of all legalism.

The Jews had erected a fence between themselves and the Gentiles. Paul tells us that Jesus made the two groups one by breaking down "the dividing wall of hostility" (Eph. 2:14). The power of the resurrected Christ has also made unnecessary any man-made defenses of the gospel.

Notwithstanding all the history to the contrary, still the doctrine of inerrancy is cherished as a protection. In his plea to those who made such a claim, Evans said: "You protest against the unsettling of faith. You do well. But they also do well who protest against keeping up needless barriers to faith."[15] It is not the purpose of this book to unsettle the faith of any Christian, but the risk must be taken in order to remove the "needless barrier" which has kept many more from exercising faith in Christ. The younger generation is alert, and in certain areas it is far more advanced for its years than was the older generation. From grade school through university young folks are acquainted with many areas of knowledge and learn to use their human reason inductively.

Yet in the last half century the primary emphasis of many groups working with high school and college students has been the inerrancy of the Bible. This was thought to be the one weapon capable of refuting the widespread belief in the doctrine of evolution. The sign of a Christian was one's courage to contest the views of the science teacher. Since "False in one, false in all" had become the slogan, one dare not admit one error in Scripture or the agnostic college student would go so far as to deny the resurrection. But for all his doubting spirit, even the sincere agnostic knew the difference between minor details and key events or teachings in Scripture. Yet to test the Christians, and in some cases to bait them, the agnostics made much of the errors they could find, all the while claiming that because Scripture was false at one point it was false everywhere. When tradition accepted this dogma it was hopelessly on the defensive. Far too often "the sons of this world are wiser in their own generation than the sons of light" (Luke 16:8).

The higher and the more rigid Christians build their fences, however, the less the real gospel gets out. Doubters are seldom inclined to have an open mind to accept any of the positive message because they see that these Christians are not being completely honest in the problem areas. Honesty, after all, is a two-way street. Those being evangelized expect Christians to present the truth all the way down the line, but when the defenders of truth fail to acknowledge the facts in areas where they can be checked, then their hearers are usually alienated. How much better it would be to acknowledge humbly some of the defects of Scripture, and then let the Holy Spirit use the "good news" in convicting the hearers.

Ultimately all fence-building results from fear. When we lose our confidence in God and his power, we go on the defensive. Instead of stressing the many portions of clear, positive teaching in Scripture, and backing up this teaching with a convincing personal witness in word and deed, we tend to save face by shoring up our weak foundations. On the other hand, when we are alive with the dynamic of Christ we are on the move. In the spiritual realm, as in the military, the best defense is a powerful offense. Or as John expressed it, "The light shines in the darkness, and the darkness has not overcome it" (John 1:5). Jesus, the Light of the world, said that his followers were to be the "light of the world" (Matt. 5:14), and that light, even though reflected, is intended to dispel the darkness.

Errancy and "Drawing the Line"

Another reason for hesitancy in renouncing the doctrine of inerrancy is the fear that there will be no means for drawing the line between truth and error. But those who hold to this line of reasoning fail to recognize that the very situation they fear theoretically is what actually faces them every time they read their Bibles seriously. The doctrine of inerrancy has to do with the autographs, and since those who hold to the doctrine do not have them, they are as dependent on extant Scriptures as are those who reject the doctrine of inerrancy.

All Christians readily acknowledge that the present manuscripts include some errors. One can say that one believes every word of extant Scripture, but this affirmation does not make every word true. One must decide which parts of the Bible are mistaken or else one is unwittingly accepting error as truth. One may think the crisis has been eluded by withholding judgment on many questions or by putting these problems in a "mystery bag," but by this very act one has removed portions of Scripture from the category of indubitable, applicable truth. Whether one realizes it or not, or whether one tries to rationalize the issue or not, everyone who believes in the validity and indispensability of Scripture is confronted with the inescapable duty of using one's rational powers to ferret out the mistaken elements in Scripture.

This very practical problem is well discussed in the following statement by Llewelyn Evans: "The Bible is a pneumatic [spiritual] Book. The groundwork, the substance, all that makes the Book what it is, is pneumatic. The warp and woof of it is pneuma. Its fringes run off, as was inevitable, into the secular, the material, the psychic. Can we not, as persons of common intelligence even, much more with the internal witness of the Spirit to aid us, discriminate between the fringe and the warp and woof? Do not the 'spiritualities' and the 'heavenlinesses' of Scripture distinguish themselves from all that is lower, as the steady shining of the everlasting stars from the fitful gleaming of earth's fireflies? Even if the task of discriminating were immeasurably harder than it is, we should not complain. God lays on us in many matters, in matters, too, of great practical moment, the responsibility of separating the things that differ. 'Why even of yourselves judge ye not what is right?' [Luke 12:57.] This responsibility is a part of life's discipline. It is not God's way to do all our thinking for us." [16]

Anyone who has experienced the regenerating power of Christ comes to Scripture with the assurance that it "has the words of eternal life." Where new evidence proves that some statement of God's Word is inaccurate, one can readily accept the fact knowing that the essential truths will never be altered. In the United States, with its Christian heritage, the individual is innocent until proved guilty. Should this not also be true of Scripture?

Inerrancy and Authority

The dire consequences of faulty reasoning used in defending inerrancy are well illustrated in the running battle between some Christian groups and science. This is not a new issue, because the seeds of the conflict were sown back in the sixteenth and seventeenth centuries. The first great scientific issue involved the relationship of our world to other planets and the sun. In quite normal, egocentric fashion the ancient world considered the earth as the center of things. The Polish astronomer Nicolaus Copernicus (1473–1543) seems to have been the first to claim, on the basis of observations and mathematical inferences, that the sun was the center of the universe. He came to this conclusion about 1525, but hesitancy as to how the edivence could most appropriately be presented resulted in delay of publication. His findings, *Revolution of the Celestial Spheres,* did not appear until 1543, the year of his death.

While the Copernican view was contrary to the mainstream of philosophical and theological thought in the sixteenth century, there was no organized opposition. In the first place, the view had not been demonstrated to be true, and secondly, many Christians were able to reconcile the new data with their previous systems of thought. The ambiguity of the situation was lessened considerably in the early decades of the seventeenth century. Johannes Kepler (1571–1630), the German astronomer and mathematician, was a major factor in this change. On the basis of careful observations of the planets and stars he was able to work up mathematical tables (published in 1627) that enabled him to make accurate astronomical predictions. Now that prediction coincided with observation there was no doubt in the minds of many that Copernicus was correct in his basic assertion.

From the standpoint of the average person the more decisive, practical confirmation of the Copernican view was the work of Galileo (1564–1642), the famous Italian astronomer. By 1609 he had built the first telescope and in the ensuing years he demonstrated, for example, that the Milky Way consisted of stars instead of vapor, and that Jupiter had bodies orbiting around it.

At the same time that the Copernican view was gaining visual and mathematical support, there was developing in theological circles a very rigid point of view. In Protestantism, both Lutheran and Reformed traditions, as well as in Roman Catholicism, the doctrine of inerrant Scripture came to be the defense employed against the inroads of science. Because the Bible spoke of the sun standing still (Josh. 10:13) and rising (Ps. 19:4-6; Matt. 5:45), the Ptolemaic theory, with the earth as the center, was the only acceptable view.

Galileo, on the contrary, contended that the Bible should not have authority over such matters as astronomy. Finally his views became so obnoxious to the ecclesiastical authorities of the Roman Catholic Church that he was brought to trial. On June 22, 1633, when approximately seventy years of age, Galileo was condemned as "vehemently suspected of heresy, namely, of having believed and held the doctrine — which is false and contrary to the sacred and divine Scriptures — that the sun is the center of the world and does not move from east to west and that the earth moves and is not the center of the world." Such pressures were brought to bear on Galileo that he paid lip service to the church by making a vocal rejection of all his views concerning the relationship of the earth and the sun. Later tradition, perhaps legendary, reports that on arising from his knees Galileo said in a soft voice, "Nevertheless it does move." Whether apocryphal or not, the statement probably expresses the true sentiments of Galileo because the Inquisition trial had not changed the facts. He was just unfortunate enough to have run afoul of the church's *interpretation* of Scripture.

Although Protestantism did not bring Roman Catholic Galileo to trial, it was inclined to condemn him by word of mouth and the printed page. Most Protestant theologians, like their Roman Catholic counterparts, quoted Biblical texts as proof that the Copernican view was a grave threat to the Christian faith. The evidence that Galileo had in his support amounted to nothing in the face of the combined prejudice of both the Western branches of Christendom. The alchemy of the church's dogmatism converted the facts into heresy.

What can the Christian church learn from this bit of history? Philip E. Hughes answers: "The lessons of the Galileo case are plain enough for those who are willing to perceive them. Absolute authoritarianism, whether in church or state, whether in theology or science, is an evil thing, and must be withstood by those who value truth and freedom and the dignity of the individual."[17] Hughes has gone to the heart of the matter: "Absolute authoritarianism . . . is an evil thing." It is evil because in quenching the truth and man's freedom to seek it the church or tradition becomes the enemy of God.

Is it any less so in the area of inspiration? When some Christians persist, contrary to the evidence, in considering their interpretations of inspiration as the clear teaching of Scripture, how do they differ in principle from the Roman Catholics in Galileo's day? The harmful effects of this modern authoritarianism need to be remedied — we need to go through our Copernican revolution in the area of inspiration. This will never happen, however, until we are willing to look through the telescope and accept what we see!

Since treasured ideas are not given up readily, the most important factor is a scrupulous honesty to know the truth, come what may. In acknowledging the error of some of his early views, John Baillie attributed part of the fault to "certain wrong-headed and illusory ideas" that he "imbibed from the spirit of the age and from the philosophies that were then in vogue."[18] He goes on to say: "What I now realize very clearly, and am ready to confess, is that much of the trouble in the days when I could not hear God's voice was that I was not really listening. I was partly listening perhaps — giving, as it were, one ear to his commandments; but no promise is made in the Bible to those who partly listen, but only to those who hearken *diligently*. And why did I not thus hearken? It was that there were certain things I did not want to hear. We sometimes speak of people being 'conveniently deaf' to human communications, but there is such a thing also as being conveniently deaf towards God; and it is a malady that afflicts us all. There are certain things we just do not want to be told. They would be too inconvenient, too upsetting, too exacting. The readjustment they would involve would be too painful. They would commit us to tasks more difficult and troublesome than we desire to undertake, or they would interfere with certain indulgences we have been allowing ourselves."[19] Admittedly, Baillie made these remarks in connection with his discussion of the difficulty which the sophisticated mind of our age poses in accepting objectively the revelation God has given. But when it comes to the matter of accepting new truth, truth that demands a painful readjustment of thought, the attitude of heart and mind is no different for the liberal than it is for the conservative. Is it not possible that devotion to the doctrine of inerrancy has tended to make its advocates conveniently deaf to the truth of the matter because of the upsetting consequences inherent in the facts?

The Copernican revolution involved in turning from the indulgence of one's own interpretation about inspiration to the facts of the Biblical teaching on inspiration may well be a traumatic experience, but through it all one can have the assurance that irrespective of one's fears the truth will always lead to Christ. Patton expressed his assurance as follows: "I like when I go to sea to know that the ship is provided with bulkheads and watertight compartments, so that in case a collision come, whether it be on bow or bilge, she will float. I do not care to put all my hope of heaven in a theory of inerrant inspiration, so that if a hole were bored in it the great ship would founder. I like to feel that the historicity and the inspiration of the Bible cooperate and help to strengthen faith, so that if either is sufficient how much better both will be." [20]

Difficult though it may be to understand, God chose to make his authority relevant to man by means which necessitate some element of fallibility. Whether we like to think of authority in such terms is beside the point. The facts permit no other understanding of Scripture's inspiration and authority. Concerning this mystery, Evans comments: "How know we what Divine, infallible, and perfect Purpose may be served even by these limitations and fallibilities? Does not Scripture itself intimate that at least there *is* such a purpose, and that it does work through just such channels of human frailty? Is not God's strength always made perfect in man's weakness? . . . If God thus chooses to work out his problems through surds and fractions and zeros, who are we to say him nay? Brethren, this is God's way; this is the law. What right have we to say where that law shall stop? to decide how much of the earthen vessel shall count as a factor? how much or how little of the human folly, weakness, nothingness, is compatible with the Divine Purpose? God is not limited as to his means and methods in communicating his will to men. Had a literal, stereotyped, incorruptible infallibility in every jot and tittle of the record been an indispensable requisite, God had a thousand resources at his command for securing such a record. That he chose men, yes, men, with all their ignorance and weakness and fallibility; that he intrusted his revelation to their stammering tongues and to their stumbling pens; that he deposited the interpretation of his eternal ways in earthen vessels, which could not escape the corruptions and mutilations of time; simply shows that a literal, particularistic infallibility is of less moment in the sight of God than some other things; of less worth, perhaps, than the thrill of a human touch, the glow of a red-hot word, the pulse of a throbbing heart, the lightning of a living eye, the flash of a soul on fire; of less worth — who knows? — than the faltering of the pilgrim's foot; dearer to heaven than the lordly step of Gabriel."[21]

We need to remind ourselves that the verbal plenary formulation of inspiration is, after all, only a doctrine — a non-Biblical doctrine at that. However, no doctrine, Biblical or non-Biblical, can ever elicit true faith. No matter how rationally or logically a doctrine may be presented, there is no guarantee that a person will take the step of faith which recognizes God's authority over him. This act of commitment comes only through the work of the Holy Spirit, and the Spirit, so history tells us, does not limit his activity only to those who believe in inerrancy.

In the last analysis, a rejection of the doctrine of inerrancy involves primarily a mental readjustment. Nothing basic is lost. In fact, when all the evidence is examined, those essential elements which the advocates of the doctrine of inerrancy have cherished and sought to protect are more firmly supported than ever before. Scripture is the product of inspiration and it is the indispensable source for coming to know God's claim upon us and his will for us.

Creed or Christ?

In life, as in death, there is only one secure place — the refuge of God's love and care. We get there by faith in Jesus Christ, not in some creed about him. Warfield said inerrancy was the last thing to be proved about Scripture, but unwittingly many earnest Christians have made it the cornerstone of their faith. They are unaware of having shifted their foundations from the rock Christ Jesus. It is little wonder, then, that so many of these Christians feel shaken and on the point of losing their faith when the doctrine of inerrancy is cleared away from under them.

It is time that all Christians make certain that their foundation is in Christ and his view of Scripture. Gnawing fears will vanish, and vision and power will take their place. We need to be about the affairs of God's Kingdom and that means being on the offensive with the proclamation of the gospel. Carl Henry has put it well: "The evangelical task primarily is the preaching of the gospel, in the interest of individual regeneration by the supernatural grace of God, in such a way that divine redemption can be recognized as the best solution of our problems, individual and social. This produces within history, through the regenerative work of the Holy Spirit, a divine society that transcends national and international lines. The corporate testimony of believers, in this purity of life, should provide for the world an example of the divine dynamic to overcome evils in every realm. The social problems of our day are much more complex than in apostolic times, but they do not on that account differ in principle. When the twentieth-century church begins to 'outlive' its environment as the first-century church outreached its pagan neighbors, the modern mind, too, will stop casting about for other solutions. The great contemporary problems are moral and spiritual. They demand more than a formula."[22] Yes, the great issues of our day demand even more than the "formula" of inerrant autographs. If we can get through this "sound barrier," as it were, without shattering too many theological windows, we will be ready to challenge the tremendous moral and spiritual problems that confront us on every side.

12: *Epilogue*

WITH THE SPECIFIC PURPOSE of reconciliation and redemption, God determined to make known his person to, and his will for, rebellious, estranged mankind. In this long process of self-disclosure he employed "many and various ways" to achieve his goal. Of primary importance were his saving acts in behalf of his covenant people. But these events in the realm of human history were more than just charades in which the spectators were left to supply their own meaning. From the call of Abraham to the birth of the church at Pentecost, the saving deeds of God were made intelligible by words of interpretation. God's communication through deeds and words found ready response in the hearts and minds of some, and at that moment revelation became an actualized reality. The chief recipients of revelation were the prophets and the apostles, but in God's variegated disclosure there was also place for artistic skills, charismatic gifts, and the wisdom of the elders.

Associated with the giving and receiving of God's revelation of himself was the divine aid (inspiration) of God's Spirit. Varying degrees of divine aid were called for by the manifold means employed by God in his self-disclosure. At those special events in God's redemptive activity the servants of God were uniquely inspired by the Spirit of God. At other times only the inspiration of a devoted Israelite or follower of Christ was necessary to achieve God's purpose. Only a general statement of the range or extent of revelation and inspiration can be given. It is neither possible nor necessary to categorize each event precisely. Suffice it to say that God's Spirit was at work in all those redemptive activities whether they come under the heading of special revelation and unique inspiration or not.

At first the witness to revelation from God was in the form of oral report. In due time some of these reports were reduced to writing, especially the key redemptive, historical events and the compelling " word of the LORD " which came to the prophets. The pattern of oral tradition followed by written records was equally true of the New Testament. In this whole process of transmitting, recording, and compiling the deeds and words of God, the Spirit of God was active in the hearts and minds of God's servants. But this activity did not extend to inerrant transmission, either oral or written, and neither did it guarantee an absolute inerrancy of the original documents. What the Spirit's activity did guarantee was selectivity of events and accuracy of reporting and interpretation sufficient to achieve God's purpose throughout the rest of man's existence.

The Scriptures, according to the traditional understanding of the church, *are* special revelation and therefore uniquely inspired. Technically speaking, however, the Bible is a record or witness to revelation, and as such it is a product of inspiration. This is not to deny the amazing accuracy, authenticity, and trustworthiness of Scripture. Rather, it is to recognize that there are two different kinds of truth. Scripture is objective truth. Since it is rooted in history, the key events of redemptive history are to be investigated and authenticated, insofar as is possible, by the same criteria employed in checking all other historical data. Man's rational faculties can also investigate the logic and meaning of the teachings in Scripture. But a thorough study of Scripture by means of unaided human reason can never lead to the act of faith. The facts and teachings of Scripture do not possess the power to coerce trust and commitment on the part of the reader. Only as God's Holy Spirit seals the message of Scripture on the heart of the reader is he ready to respond and make revelation an actuality by exercising his will in an act of commitment to God.

Subjective truth has to do with reasons of the heart, whereas objective truth has to do with reasons of the mind. At any given moment a person cannot be actively engaged in both realms of truth, but this does not mean that the two are antithetical. As Brunner observes: "The relation between the two kinds of truth is the same as that between the planes of existence: the higher includes the lower, but not vice versa. The personal truth of revelation, faith, and love includes within itself the impersonal truth connected with 'things,' and the impersonal truth connected with abstractions, but not vice versa."[1] Objective truth of itself cannot guarantee the reality of subjective truth, but subjective truth cannot occur without some minimal amount of objective truth. The Holy Spirit works in conjunction with the reading, preaching, and teaching of Scripture; therefore the objective truth of the Biblical record is neglected or rejected at the peril of one's spiritual well-being.

True faith, therefore, is more than a blind leap into the dark. It begins in the area of objective truth with assent to the facts and teachings of Scripture. Otherwise the act of faith would amount to a credulous will to believe — a game of chance. The objective truth of natural revelation and of Scripture serve as the springboard of faith because they point in the direction in which one is to exercise his faith. Nevertheless the act of trust and commitment into the loving arms of the Father is made only at the level of subjective, personal truth.

Thus in the Christian's walk with Christ it is a case of both objective and subjective truth. While the Christian experience, like true marriage, loses its dynamic without repeated experiences of subjective truth, it is by no means a continuous state of rapture, transport, or ecstasy. Rather, it is an alternation between the objective and subjective aspects of life. True worship may begin with objective truth (meditation about God), but it should go on to subjective truth (being "lost in wonder, love, and praise").

The two kinds of truth are equally valid in the realm of authority. The ultimate authority of God's sovereignty was expressed in terms of specific demands upon his covenant people.

His will was made increasingly clear throughout the long period of progressive revelation, the culmination being the total ministry of Jesus Christ. Today God expresses his will through Scripture, the record of revelation. It is the only source for determining what God requires of us, but it was written over many centuries in an ancient, Oriental culture of the Near East, and many of its regulations and customs do not apply now. By proper methods of interpretation human reason can distill the relevant aspects of Scripture, but this exercise in the realm of objective truth does not make the ascertained will of God authoritative. The conviction that leads to submission and obedience comes only through the wooing of the Holy Spirit. In the subjective truth of personal encounter, God's will is made clear and authoritative. Each person will be judged according to his willingness to know God's will and the extent of his obedience to that will. In fact, then, recognition of ultimate authority is an individual, personal matter and one cannot superimpose one's own convictions upon another.

In all essential matters of faith and practice Scripture is authentic, accurate, and trustworthy. It is the indispensable record of revelation, product of inspiration, and source of authority. By Scripture, and it alone, revelation, inspiration, and authority become subjective truth in every earnest heart through the agency of the same Spirit who watched over Scripture's recording and transmission. This result occurs whether Scripture is in the original languages or in translation. Of course, for clarification of specific details, the best extant text of the Hebrew and Aramaic in the Old Testament and the Greek in the New Testament will always have a priority over any translations. But in the great issues of faith (love for God) and action (love for man) Scripture in translation is sufficient to achieve God's purpose. This is true of all translations even though they have unintentional, and in some cases deliberate, variation from the clear text of the extant manuscripts. As far as the translation itself is concerned, and indirectly the reader, the reason for the variation does not matter. Enough of the redemptive truth is woven throughout

Scripture that the Holy Spirit can take any translation and use it for the salvation of the sincere reader.

The whole history of God's redemptive activity is one in which the Holy Spirit has worked through imperfect means, both men and Scripture, without the means being a handicap. Fallible ministers with many imperfect notions have been God's messengers throughout the history of the church. In spite of this fact the "hungry and thirsty" have heard them gladly as being inspired by God and setting forth a trustworthy message. If the Holy Spirit is willing to authenticate the message of very fallible servants, how much more will he authenticate the extant manuscripts and translations!

NOTES

Notes

Chapter 2. Inspiration and the Autographs

1. See Warfield, *The Inspiration and Authority of the Bible,* pp. 245–296. Quotations from this book are used by permission of Presbyterian & Reformed Publishing Co.

2. See Van Til, " Introduction " to Warfield, *The Inspiration and Authority of the Bible,* p. 46, note 22.

3. R. Laird Harris, *Inspiration and Canonicity of the Bible,* p. 103.

4. See Unger, " H. H. Rowley and the New Trend in Biblical Studies," *Inspiration and Interpretation,* ed. by Walvoord, pp. 197–198.

Chapter 3. Transmission, Translation, and Inspiration

1. Henry, *Commentary on the Whole Bible,* Vol. II, p. 858. Italics his.

2. See Warfield and Hodge, *Inspiration,* pp. 14, 16. Reprinted from *Presbyterian Review,* April, 1881.

3. Orr, *Revelation and Inspiration,* p. 165. Italics his. Quotations from this book are used by permission of Wm. B. Eerdmans Publishing Company.

4. See Edward F. Hills, *The King James Version Defended!* pp. 25, 27, 114–116, 122, 141.

5. Quenstedt, *Theologia Didactico-Polemica sive Systema Theologicum,* I, 206.

6. Preus, *The Inspiration of Scripture,* p. 49.

7. See Edward J. Young, *Thy Word Is Truth,* pp. 55–56.

8. See, e.g., Robert Dick Wilson *Studies in the Book of Daniel,* Vol. I, p. 85.

9. *Aristeas to Philocrates* (*Letter of Aristeas*), ed. and tr. by Moses Hadas, p. 219.
10. *Ibid.*, p. 221.
11. Philo, *Life of Moses*, Book II, par. 37, as tr. by F. H. Colson, *Philo with an English Translation*, Vol. VI, p. 467.
12. *Ibid.*, pars. 38–40, pp. 467, 469.
13. See, e.g., R. Laird Harris, *Inspiration and Canonicity of the Bible*, p. 100.
14. Augustine, Letter 82, p. 392, in *Augustine, Letters* (*1–82*), Vol. 12, The Fathers of the Church.
15. Augustine, *Christian Instruction*, Book 2, Ch. 15, p. 80, in Vol. 2, The Fathers of the Church.

Chapter 4. Inerrancy and the Phenomena of Scripture

1. Carnell, *The Case for Orthodox Theology*, pp. 98–99.
2. Orr, *Revelation and Inspiration*, p. 180.
3. Thiele, *The Mysterious Numbers of the Hebrew Kings*, p. 114.
4. *Ibid.*, p. 268.
5. Brunner, *Revelation and Reason*, p. 275.
6. Harrison, "The Phenomena of Scripture," *Revelation and the Bible*, p. 239.
7. Henry, *Commentary on the Whole Bible*, Vol. VI, p. 80.
8. Bruce, *Commentary on the Book of Acts, The New International Commentary on the New Testament*, p. 149, note 39.
9. Carnell, *op. cit.*, pp. 102–103.
10. Harrison, "Criteria of Biblical Inerrancy," *Christianity Today*, Vol. II, No. 8 (Jan. 20, 1958), p. 16.
11. Evans, *Inspiration and Inerrancy*, pp. 30–31. Italics his.
12. Patton, *Fundamental Christianity*, pp. 146–147.
13. *Ibid.*, pp. 163–164.
14. Glueck, *Horizon*, Vol. II, No. 2 (November, 1959), p. 6.
15. *Ibid.*
16. *Ibid.*

Chapter 5. Verbal Inspiration

1. Preus, *The Inspiration of Scripture*, p. 33.
2. Orr, *Revelation and Inspiration*, p. 162.
3. Preus, *op. cit.*, p. 22.
4. *Ibid.*, p. 174.

5. Baillie, *The Idea of Revelation in Recent Thought,* p. 116. Quotations from this book are used by permission of the publisher, Columbia University Press.

6. Westcott, *An Introduction to the Study of the Gospels,* p. 14.

7. Kantzer, "Calvin and the Holy Scriptures," *Inspiration and Interpretation,* p. 147.

8. Calvin, *Commentary on a Harmony of the Evangelists, Matthew, Mark, and Luke,* tr. by William Pringle, Vol. III, p. 10.

9. Preus, *op. cit.,* pp. 196–197.

Chapter 6. Plenary Inspiration and the Canon

1. Preus, *The Inspiration of Scripture,* p. 83.

2. See Harris, *Inspiration and Canonicity of the Bible,* pp. 167–174.

3. Charles, ed., *The Apocrypha and Pseudepigrapha of the Old Testament in English,* Vol. II, p. 622.

4. *Ibid.,* pp. 623–624.

5. Epstein, ed., *The Babylonian Talmud,* Vol. 10, Megillah 7b, p. 36.

6. *Ibid.,* p. 35.

7. *Ibid.,* p. 38.

8. See Edward J. Young, *An Introduction to the Old Testament,* p. 340.

9. See Unger, *Introductory Guide to the Old Testament,* p. 390.

10. See Davidson, ed., *The New Bible Commentary,* p. 539.

11. Epstein, *op cit.,* Vol. 3, Shabbath 30b, p. 135.

12. See Warfield, *The Inspiration and Authority of the Bible,* pp. 415–416.

13. Jaak Seynaeve, *Cardinal Newman's Doctrine on Holy Scripture,* pp. 50*–51* in Appendices, "Newman Manuscripts on Holy Scripture," No. III, "On the Connection in Doctrine and Statement of the Books of the Apocrypha with the New Testament" (Anglican period — date unknown). Italics his.

Chapter 7. Tradition and Inspiration

1. See Warfield, *The Inspiration and Authority of the Bible,* p. 106.

2. Philo, *Life of Moses,* Book II, par. 34, as tr. by F. H. Colson, *Philo with an English Translation,* Vol. VI, p. 465.

3. *Ibid.*, par. 37, p. 467.
4. Wolfson, *Philo,* Vol. I, p. 116.
5. *Ibid.*, p. 120.
6. *Ibid.*, p. 124.
7. *Ibid.*, p. 125.
8. Justin Martyr, Apology I, ch. 36, p. 38, and Hortatory Address, ch. 35, p. 323, *The Writings of Justin Martyr and Athenagoras,* Vol. II, Ante-Nicene Christian Library.
9. Athenagoras, ch. IX, *ibid.*, p. 384.
10. See, e.g., J. Barton Payne, "The Biblical Interpretation of Irenaeus," *Inspiration and Interpretation,* p. 21.
11. Tertullian, *Apology,* ch. 18, par. 2, pp. 53–54, in *Tertullian, Apologetical Works,* Vol. 10, The Fathers of the Church.
12. Origen, Homily XXXIX, in Jeremiah, p. 50, *Selections from the Commentaries and Homilies of Origen,* tr. by R. B. Tollinton.
13. Origen, Commentary in John, X. 3, *ibid.*, p. 107.
14. Westcott, "Appendix B. On the Primitive Doctrine of Inspiration," p. 455, *An Introduction to the Study of the Gospels.* Italics his.
15. *Ibid.*, p. 456. Italics his.
16. Harbison, *The Christian Scholar in the Age of the Reformation,* pp. 18–19. Italics his.
17. Augustine, Letter 82, p. 392, in *Augustine, Letters (1–82),* Vol. 12, The Fathers of the Church.
18. Augustine, *Christian Instruction,* Book 2, ch. 16, p. 85 in Vol 2, The Fathers of the Church.
19. Luther, *Sämmtliche Schriften,* edited by Johann Georg Walch, St. Louis Edition, IX:87.
20. Quenstedt, *Theologia Didactico-Polemica sive Systema Theologicum,* I, 112.
21. Gaussen, *The Inspiration of the Holy Scriptures,* p. 34.
22. *Ibid.*, p. 29.
23. Warfield, *op. cit.*, p. 420.
24. Young, *Thy Word Is Truth,* p. 27.
25. Hebert, *The Authority of the Old Testament,* p. 98.
26. R. A. Finlayson, "Contemporary Ideas of Inspiration," *Revelation and the Bible,* p. 233.
27. Warfield and Hodge, *Inspiration,* p. 5.

Chapter 8. Revelation, Inspiration, and Existentialism

1. Kierkegaard, *Concluding Unscientific Postscript,* p. 178. In the source the entire quotation is in italics.
2. *Ibid.,* p. 181. Italics his.
3. *Ibid.,* pp. 179–180.
4. Orr, *Revelation and Inspiration,* p. 197.
5. Brunner, *Revelation and Reason,* p. 9.
6. *Ibid.,* p. 8. Italics his.
7. Barth, *Church Dogmatics,* Vol. I, Part 2, p. 522. Quotations from this book are used by permission of Charles Scribner's Sons and T. & T. Clark.
8. *Ibid.,* p. 533.
9. *Ibid.,* p. 532.
10. *Ibid.,* p. 530.
11. *Ibid.,* p. 533.
12. *Ibid.,* p. 525.
13. *Ibid.,* pp. 529–530.
14. *Ibid.,* pp. 533–534.
15. *Ibid.,* p. 544.
16. Strong, *Systematic Theology,* p. 196.

Chapter 9. Revelation, Inspiration, and Doctrine

1. Warfield and Hodge, *Inspiration,* p. 5.
2. *Ibid.,* pp. 5–6.
3. Orr, *Revelation and Inspiration,* pp. 197–198.
4. Sanday, *Inspiration,* p. 398.
5. Hebert, *The Authority of the Old Testament,* p. 103.
6. Curtis, *The Christian Faith,* p. 177.
7. *Ibid.,* p. 178.
8. *Ibid.,* pp. 178–179.
9. Orr, *op. cit.,* p. 177. Italics his.
10. *Ibid.,* p. 178.
11. Bailey, *The Gospel in Hymns,* p. 459.
12. Temple, *Nature, Man and God,* p. 354.
13. Baillie, *The Idea of Revelation in Recent Thought,* pp. 27, 28.
14. Dodd, *The Authority of the Bible,* p. 294.
15. Brunner, *Revelation and Reason,* p. 8.
16. Baillie, *op. cit.,* p. 29.
17. Brunner, *op. cit.,* p. 367.

18. *Ibid.*, p. 366. Italics his.
19. *Ibid.*, p. 367. Italics his.
20. *Ibid.*, pp. 371–372. Italics his.
21. *Ibid.*, p. 420.
22. *Ibid.*, pp. 419–420.
23. *Ibid.*, p. 421.
24. Forsyth, *The Principle of Authority*, p. 452.
25. Brunner, *op. cit.*, pp. 369–370.

Chapter 10. Revelation, Inspiration, and Fact

1. Pfeiffer, "Facts and Faith in Biblical History," *Journal of Biblical Literature*, Vol. LXX, Part I (March, 1951), p. 10.
2. *Ibid.*, p. 13.
3. *Ibid.*, p. 14.
4. Owen, *Revelation and Existence*, pp. 25–26. Italics his.
5. *Ibid.*, pp. 27–28. Italics his.
6. Niebuhr, R. R., *Resurrection and Historical Reason*, p. 48.
7. Brunner, *Revelation and Reason*, p. 281.
8. *Ibid.*, pp. 281–282.
9. *Ibid.*, p. 282.
10. Niebuhr, *op. cit.*, p. 27.
11. Barth, *Church Dogmatics*, Vol. I, Part 2, p. 184.
12. Lewis, *Miracles*, p. 165.
13. Machen, *The Virgin Birth of Christ*, p. 395.
14. *Ibid.*, pp. 395–396.
15. *Ibid.*, p. 396.
16. Albright, *The Archaeology of Palestine*, pp. 242–243.
17. Albright, "Recent Discoveries in Palestine and the Gospel of St. John," *The Background of the New Testament and Its Eschatology*, pp. 153–170.
18. Montgomery, *The Origin of the Gospel According to St. John*, p. 30, quoted by Albright, *ibid.*, p. 171.
19. Albright, *The Archaeology of Palestine*, p. 248.

Chapter 11. Inerrancy, Doctrine, Security, and Authority

1. Cornelius Van Til, "Introduction" to Warfield, *The Inspiration and Authority of the Bible*, p. 66.
2. Henry C. Thiessen, *An Introduction to the New Testament*, p. 80.

3. Edward J. Young, *Thy Word Is Truth,* p. 73.
4. *Ibid.,* p. 86.
5. Evans, "Biblical Scholarship and Inspiration," *Inspiration and Inerrancy,* p. 70.
6. Jewett, "Special Revelation as Historical and Personal," *Revelation and the Bible,* p. 52.
7. Packer, *"Fundamentalism" and the Word of God,* p. 129.
8. Warfield, *The Inspiration and Authority of the Bible,* p. 210.
9. *Ibid.,* p. 211.
10. Henry, *The Protestant Dilemma,* p. 82.
11. Warfield, *op. cit.,* p. 162.
12. Ramm, *The Christian View of Science and Scripture,* p. 29.
13. Ladd, *The Blessed Hope,* p. 53.
14. *Ibid.*
15. Evans, *op. cit.,* p. 86.
16. *Ibid.,* pp. 81–82.
17. Hughes, *Christianity Today,* Vol. IV, No. 8 (Jan. 18, 1960), p. 34.
18. Baillie, *The Idea of Revelation in Recent Thought,* p. 141.
19. *Ibid.,* p. 140. Italics his.
20. Patton, *Fundamental Christianity,* pp. 165–166.
21. Evans, *op. cit.,* pp. 40–41.
22. Henry, *The Uneasy Conscience of Modern Fundamentalism,* p. 88.

Chapter 12. Epilogue

1. Brunner, *Revelation and Reason,* p. 373.

BIBLIOGRAPHY

Bibliography

In addition to the books and articles cited in the notes the bibliography lists other sources consulted.

Albright, William F., *The Archaeology of Palestine* (Harmondsworth-Middlesex, 1949).

——— " Recent Discoveries in Palestine and the Gospel of St. John," *The Background of the New Testament and Its Eschatology,* ed. by W. D. Davies and D. Daube (Cambridge University Press, Cambridge, 1956).

Aristeas, *Aristeas to Philocrates* (*Letter of Aristeas*), ed. and tr. by Moses Hadas (Harper & Row Publishers, Inc., 1951).

Athenagoras, *The Writings of Justin Martyr and Athenagoras,* Vol. II, Ante-Nicene Christian Library, tr. by Marcus Dods, George Reith, and B. P. Pratten (T. & T. Clark, Edinburgh, 1867).

Augustine, *Christian Instruction,* tr. by John J. Gavigan, O.S.A., Vol. 2, The Fathers of the Church (Fathers of the Church, Inc., 2d ed. 1950).

——— *Letters* (*1–82*), tr. by Wilfrid Parsons, Vol. 12, The Fathers of the Church (Fathers of the Church, Inc., 1951).

Bailey, Albert Edward, *The Gospel in Hymns* (Charles Scribner's Sons, 1950).

Baillie, John, *The Idea of Revelation in Recent Thought* (Columbia University Press, 1956).

Barth, Karl, *The Doctrine of the Word of God,* Vol. I, Part 1, *Church Dogmatics,* tr. by G. T. Thomson (Charles Scribner's Sons, and T. & T. Clark, 1936).

——— *The Doctrine of the Word of God,* Vol. I, Part 2, *Church*

Dogmatics, tr. by G. T. Thomson and Harold Knight (Charles Scribner's Sons and T. & T. Clark, 1956).

Bavinck, Herman, *The Philosophy of Revelation* (Longmans, Green and Co., Inc., 1909).

Berkouwer, G. C., *General Revelation* (Wm. B. Eerdmans Publishing Company, 1955).

Briggs, Charles A., *The Bible, the Church and the Reason* (Charles Scribner's Sons, 1893).

Bruce, Alexander B., *The Chief End of Revelation* (Hodder and Stoughton, Ltd., London, 1896).

Bruce, F. F., *Commentary on the Book of the Acts, The New International Commentary on the New Testament* (Wm. B. Eerdmans Publishing Company, 1954).

Brunner, Emil, *Revelation and Reason,* tr. by Olive Wyon (The Westminster Press, 1946).

Bultmann, Rudolf, *Jesus Christ and Mythology* (Charles Scribner's Sons, 1958).

Burnaby, John, *Is the Bible Inspired?* No. 9, Colet Library Series (Gerald Duckworth and Company, Ltd., London, 1949).

Calvin, John, *Commentary on a Harmony of the Evangelists, Matthew, Mark, and Luke,* tr. by William Pringle, 3 vols. (Calvin Translation Society, Edinburgh, 1846).

——— *Commentaries on the Book of the Prophet Jeremiah and the Lamentations,* 5 vols., tr. by John Owen (Calvin Translation Society, Edinburgh, 1854).

Carnell, Edward J., *The Case for Orthodox Theology* (The Westminster Press, 1959).

Charles, R. H., ed., *The Apocrypha and Pseudepigrapha of the Old Testament in English,* 2 vols. (Clarendon Press, Oxford, 1913).

Clark, Gordon H., *Religion, Reason and Revelation* (Presbyterian and Reformed Publishing Company, 1961).

Coleridge, Samuel T., *Confessions of an Inquiring Spirit* (Adam & Charles Black, Ltd., London, 1956).

Cunliffe-Jones, Hubert, *The Authority of the Biblical Revelation* (The Pilgrim Press, 1948).

Curtis, Olin A., *The Christian Faith* (Eaton & Mains, 1905).

Dillenberger, John, *Protestant Thought and Natural Science* (Doubleday & Co., Inc., 1960).

Dodd, C. H., *The Authority of the Bible* (Harper & Row, Publishers, Inc., 1929).

Epstein, I., ed., *The Babylonian Talmud,* 34 vols. plus index volume (The Soncino Press, Ltd., London, 1935, 1936, 1938, 1948, and 1952).

Evans, Llewelyn J., " Biblical Scholarship and Inspiration," pp. 25–87, *Inspiration and Inerrancy,* Henry P. Smith (Robert Clarke and Co., 1893).

Farrer, Austin, *The Glass of Vision* (The Dacre Press, 1948).

Filson, Floyd V., *Which Books Belong in the Bible?* (The Westminster Press, 1957).

Forsyth, P. T., *The Principle of Authority* (Hodder and Stoughton, Ltd., n.d.).

Gaussen, Louis, *The Inspiration of the Holy Scriptures,* tr. by David D. Scott (The Moody Press, 1949).

Gladstone, William E., *The Impregnable Rock of Holy Scripture* (John D. Wattles, 1898).

Glueck, Nelson, " The Bible as Divining Rod," *Horizon,* Vol. II, No. 2, November, 1959, pp. 4–10, 118–119.

Harbison, E. Harris, *The Christian Scholar in the Age of the Reformation* (Charles Scribner's Sons, 1956).

Harris, R. Laird, *Inspiration and Canonicity of the Bible* (Zondervan Publishing House, 1957).

Harrison, Everett F., " Criteria of Biblical Inerrancy," *Christianity Today,* Vol. II, No. 8, Jan. 20, 1958.

Hebert, A. Gabriel, *The Authority of the Old Testament* (Faber & Faber, Ltd., London, 1947).

——— *Fundamentalism and the Church* (The Westminster Press, 1957).

Henry, Carl F. H., *The Protestant Dilemma* (Wm. B. Eerdmans Publishing Company, 1949).

——— ed., *Revelation and the Bible* (Baker Book House, 1958).

——— *The Uneasy Conscience of Modern Fundamentalism* (Wm. B. Eerdmans Publishing Company, 1947).

Henry, Matthew, *Commentary on the Whole Bible,* 6 vols. (Fleming H. Revell Company, 1935).

Hills, Edward F., *The King James Version Defended!* (The Christian Research Press, 1956).

Hughes, Philip E., review of *The Crime of Galileo,* Giorgio de Santillana, in *Christianity Today,* Vol. IV, No. 8, Jan. 18, 1960, pp. 33–34.

Justin Martyr, see Martyr, Justin.

Kierkegaard, Søren, *Concluding Unscientific Postscript,* tr. by David F. Swenson with Introduction and Notes by Walter Lowrie (Princeton University Press, 1941).

Ladd, George Eldon, *The Blessed Hope* (Wm. B. Eerdmans Publishing Company, 1956).

Lewis, C. S., *Miracles* (Geoffrey Bles, Ltd., London, 1952).

Lewis, Edwin, *The Biblical Faith and Christian Freedom* (The Westminster Press, 1953).

——— *A Philosophy of the Christian Revelation* (Harper & Row, Publishers, Inc., 1940).

Machen, J. Gresham, *The Virgin Birth of Christ* (Harper & Row, Publishers, Inc., 1930).

Martyr, Justin, *The Writings of Justin Martyr and Athenagoras,* Vol. II, Ante-Nicene Christian Library, tr. by Marcus Dods, George Reith, and B. P. Pratten (T. & T. Clark, Edinburgh, 1867).

Metzger, Bruce M., *An Introduction to the Apocrypha* (Oxford University Press, 1957).

Mowinckel, Sigmund, *The Old Testament as Word of God,* tr. by Reidar B. Bjornard (Abingdon Press, 1959).

Niebuhr, H. Richard, *The Meaning of Revelation* (The Macmillan Company, 1952).

Niebuhr, Richard Reinhold, *Resurrection and Historical Reason* (Charles Scribner's Sons, 1957).

Origen, *Selections from the Commentaries and Homilies of Origen,* tr. by R. B. Tollinton (S.P.C.K., London, 1929).

Orr, James, *Revelation and Inspiration* (Wm. B. Eerdmans Publishing Company, 1952).

Owen, H. P., *Revelation and Existence* (University of Wales Press, Cardiff, 1957).

Packer, James I., *"Fundamentalism" and the Word of God* (Inter-Varsity Fellowship, London, 1958).

Patton, Francis L., *Fundamental Christianity* (The Macmillan Company, 1929).

Pfeiffer, Robert H., "Facts and Faith in Biblical History," *Journal of Biblical Literature,* Vol. LXX, Part I, March 1951, pp. 1–14.

Philo, *Life of Moses,* Book II, tr. by F. H. Colson in Vol. VI, *Philo with an English Translation,* Loeb Classical Library, Harvard University Press, 1935).

Preus, Robert, *The Inspiration of Scripture* (Oliver and Boyd Ltd., Edinburgh and London, 1955).

Quenstedt, J. A. *Theologia Didactico-Polemica sive Systema Theologicum* (Lipsiae, 1715).

Ramm, Bernard, *The Christian View of Science and Scripture* (Wm. B. Eerdmans Publishing Company, 1955).

——— *Special Revelation and the Word of God* (Wm. B. Eerdmans Publishing Company, 1961).

Reid, John K. S., *The Authority of Scripture* (Harper & Row, Publishers, Inc., 1957).

Richardson, Alan, *Christian Apologetics* (Harper & Row, Publishers, Inc., 1947).

Robinson, Henry Wheeler, *Inspiration and Revelation in the Old Testament* (Clarendon Press, Oxford, 1946).

Runia, Klaas, *Karl Barth's Doctrine of Holy Scripture* (Wm. B. Eerdmans Publishing Company, 1962).

Sanday, William, *Inspiration,* Bampton Lectures, 1893 (Longmans, Green and Co., Ltd., London, 3d ed. 1903).

Sauer, Erich, *From Eternity to Eternity — An Outline of the Divine Purposes,* tr. by G. H. Lang (Wm. B. Eerdmans Publishing Company, 1954).

Seeberg, Reinhold, *Revelation and Inspiration* (Harper & Row, Publishers, Inc., 1909).

Seynaeve, Jaak, *Cardinal Newman's Doctrine on Holy Scripture* (Universitas Catholica Lovaniensis, Series II, Tomus 45, Publications universitaires de Louvain, Louvain, 1953).

Smith, Henry Preserved, *Inspiration and Inerrancy — A History and a Defense* (Robert Clarke and Co., 1893).

Smyth, J. Paterson, *How God Inspired the Bible* (James Pott & Co., 1893).

Snaith, Norman H., *The Inspiration and Authority of the Bible* (The Epworth Press, London, 1956).

Stonehouse, Ned B., and Woolley, Paul, eds., *The Infallible Word* (Presbyterian Guardian Publication Corporation, 1946).

Strong, Augustus Hopkins, *Systematic Theology* (American Baptist Publication Society, 1907).

Tasker, R. V. G., *The Old Testament in the New Testament* (S.C.M. Press Ltd., London, 2d ed. 1954).

Temple, William, *Nature, Man and God* (The Macmillan Company, London, 1934).

Tertullian, *Apology,* tr. by Emily J. Daly, C.S.J., in *Tertullian, Apologetical Works,* Vol. 10, The Fathers of the Church (Fathers of the Church, Inc., 1950).

Thiele, Edwin R., *The Mysterious Numbers of the Hebrew Kings* (University of Chicago Press, 1951).

Thiessen, Henry Clarence, *Introduction to the New Testament* (Wm. B. Eerdmans Publishing Company, 3d ed., 1943).

Tillich, Paul, *Systematic Theology,* Vol. I (University of Chicago Press, 1951).

Unger, Merrill F., *Introductory Guide to the Old Testament* (Zondervan Publishing House, 1951).

Van Til, Cornelius, "Introduction," pp. 3–68, in Warfield, *The Inspiration and Authority of the Bible,* ed. by Samuel G. Craig.

Walvoord, John F., ed., *Inspiration and Interpretation* (Wm. B. Eerdmans Publishing Company, 1957).

Warfield, Benjamin B., *Biblical and Theological Studies,* edited by Samuel G. Craig (Presbyterian and Reformed Publishing Company, 1952).

Warfield, Benjamin B., and Hodge, Archibald A., *Inspiration* (Philadelphia, n.d., reprinted from *Presbyterian Review,* April, 1881).

Warfield, Benjamin B., *The Inspiration and Authority of the Bible,* ed. by Samuel G. Craig (Presbyterian and Reformed Publishing Company, 1948).

Westcott, Brooke Foss, *An Introduction to the Study of the Gospels* (The Macmillan Company, 1895).

Wilson, Robert Dick, *Studies in the Book of Daniel — A Discussion of the Historical Questions* (G. P. Putnam's Sons, Knickerbocker Press, 1917).

Wolfson, Harry Austryn, *Philo,* 2 vols. (Harvard University Press, 1947).

Young, Edward J., *An Introduction to the Old Testament* (Wm. B. Eerdmans Publishing Company, 1952).

——— *Thy Word Is Truth* (Wm. B. Eerdmans Publishing Company, 1957).

INDEX

General Index

Scriptural Index

OLD TESTAMENT

APOCRYPHA

NEW TESTAMENT